TOM LOWENSTEIN worked with storyɩ 1973 and 1988. He now lives in London with his partner and two daughters. He is currently working on a study of contact in the nineteenth century between Point Hope Inuit and Euro-Americans.

"A dazzling work"
FRANCIS SPUFFORD,
London Review of Books

"A feat of poetic empathy"
MICHAEL HAMBURGER

Also by Tom Lowenstein

TOM LOWENSTEIN

Ancient Land: Sacred Whale

The Inuit Hunt, its Rituals and Poetry

THE HARVILL PRESS
LONDON

First published in Great Britain by Bloomsbury Publishing Ltd in 1993

This paperback edition first published in 1999 by
The Harvill Press
2 Aztec Row
Berners Road
London N1 0PW

1 3 5 7 9 8 6 4 2

www.harvill-press.com

Copyright © Tom Lowenstein, 1993

Tom Lowenstein asserts the moral right to be
identified as the author of this work

A CIP catalogue record for this book
is available from the British Library

ISBN 1 86046 575 7

Designed and typeset in Galliard at
Libanus Press, Marlborough, Wiltshire

Printed and bound in Great Britain by Biddles Ltd
Guildford and Kings Lynn

CONTENTS

For Niġuvana पुष्प

ACKNOWLEDGEMENTS

So much of the material in Part Two of this book derives from Froelich Rainey's fieldwork in 1940 that it is impossible to overestimate my debt. Rainey's initial work in Tikigaq (Point Hope) was the discovery and excavation of the celebrated proto-Inuit Ipiutak site in 1939. In 1940 he returned to record ethnographies from the village elders. Without his monograph, *The Whale Hunters of Tigara* (New York, 1947), my own work would have been out of the question. But the monograph uses only a fraction of the data Rainey recorded, and for much of Part Two of the present book the main source for my account of the ritual order has been Rainey's unpublished field notes. Readers who compare the present version with the monograph may notice one or two discrepancies, such as in the ordering of ceremonial house rituals. Rainey's informants themselves differed on a number of issues, partly because they came from different ceremonial groups, partly because they themselves were reconstructing a system that had been largely abandoned forty years previously. I hope my own reconstruction of the exalted fantasia of the qalgi rituals has not distorted or deformed the unknowable real thing. In the course of my acquaintance with the 1940 notes, I have grown to know and love the old-timers with whom Rainey worked, some of whose children I met as elders in the 1970s. Rainey's principal informants were Agviqsiina, Ququk, Quwana, Niguvana, Nasugluk, Nasugruk, Uyagaq, Kunuyaq, Aiviqsiq and my own storyteller and principal informant, Asatchaq Jimmie Killigivuk (1891–1980). May they be honoured.

My parallel debt is of course to the community of Point Hope, Alaska, where I worked off and on between 1973 and 1989. In addition to Asatchaq and Tukummiq, whose stories and translations are represented here, I worked over many field trips with other Tikigaq elders who became close friends for more than a decade. Principally these were Augustus and Walter Kowunna, Solomon Killigivuk, Donald and Lily Oktollik, Patrick Attungana, Kirk Oviok and Alec Millik. Also George Omnik, Charles Sagana and Lucy Ayagiiyaq Jensen, Laurie Uyagaaluk Kingik, Beatrice Maligiin Vincent, Qimiuraq Bob Tuckfield and Herbert Kinneavauk who have died within the past fifteen years. I should also especially like to thank the following friends, with whom I lived, worked and ate, or accompanied on the whale hunt: Elijah and Dorcas Rock,

Henry Nashookpuk, Joe and Lucy Towkshjea, Amos and Suuyuk Lane, Konrad Killigivuk, Isaac Killigivuk, the late Chester Killigivuk, Rex and Piquk Tuzroyluk, Willie Omnik, James Omnik, John and Mollie Oktollik.

This book has seen many transformations. It originated in 1980 with an unpublished report commissioned by the Inupiaq North Slope Borough. I wrote this twice, but for the present book I salvaged only the title and a version of the first chapter. To Karla Kolash, who commissioned the original, I remain greatly indebted.

Had I taken my cue from Tikigaq, I would have worked on the first and second versions in less isolation. The present writing was made sociable by happy circumstances in London. A semi-dramatised version of selected parts was broadcast in 1990 by BBC Radio 3, and I am grateful to Tim Suter, Joan Griffiths, and to Malcolm Clarke of the Radiophonics Workshop for bringing that to reality. I have also had the pleasure of readers along the way. Nigel Wheale, Martin Thom and Peter Riley devoted their extraordinary textual expertise to early drafts and helped pull many passages out of the wool. W. G. Shepherd and Michael Butler also read sections of Part Two and responded helpfully and in detail. John Welch and Martha Kapos were a reassuring audience over a number of readings. Last, but not least, I must thank Liz Calder of Bloomsbury, who saw the point of the book while it was in embryo. To these friends and colleagues I extend my warmest gratitude.

Tom Lowenstein
London, 1992

Tikigaq: a brief chronology

*c.*1–500 AD	Pre-Inuit Ipiutak people colonise the south shore of the Point.
600–800	Whale hunting is made possible by the introduction of harpoon and drag-float technology.
1850–1916	Commercial whalers hunt the bowhead whale for baleen (whalebone).
1890	Arrival of John D. Driggs, Tikigaq's first missionary.
1900–1910	Final period of *qalgi* rituals.

INTRODUCTION

This book is about an Inuit people of north Alaska and the whales they worshipped and killed before the white man arrived in the nineteenth century. It is about an ancient village of North America, an old sacred place, where ritual and myth kept people at peace and in living contact with the animals they hunted.

The whale was the bowhead which migrates each spring to its feeding grounds off north Alaska. The place is Tikigaq, the furthest north-west point of North America, and the oldest continuously settled native American site on the continent.

Lying on a long spit of gravel, only just above the sea, Tikigaq clings to the tip of the peninsula jutting west into the Arctic Ocean. For eight months each year Tikigaq is locked in by sea-ice; swept constantly by brutal winds, it is almost always very cold.

But Tikigaq was never desolate to the people who lived on the Point. Its hunting grounds were rich, and its earth was crowded with driftwood and whalebone iglus dug into the surface; here family life was warm and social life vivid. Perhaps less a village than a nation which controlled huge tracts of coast and inland territory, Tikigaq was also a ritual metropolis, famous among Inuit for its unique ceremonials.

This book focuses on Tikigaq earth, and the myths and rituals that explained the supernatural genesis of the peninsula. Tikigaq, said the myth, was once a whale-like creature. Killed by a primal shamanic harpooner, the whale lived on – part body, part spirit – and became the peninsula. When Tikigaq hunters (*umialik*) took whales in the spring, the whales' bodies – dismembered, and stored underground in abandoned iglus – joined the mythic whale's body.

Sustaining this myth, men and women conducted a series of astonishing rituals. These constituted a long, extended drama, so numerous and elaborate in its parts, that they filled the entirety of spring and autumn. Part II of this book is an account of these rituals.

I started work in the village in 1973, when the whale myth had all but died and whale-hunting lore had broken under the stress of culture contact. But certain men and women born before this century still lived within the realm of mythological thought. Recording their stories and exploring the local territory, I began to grasp how the stories had been

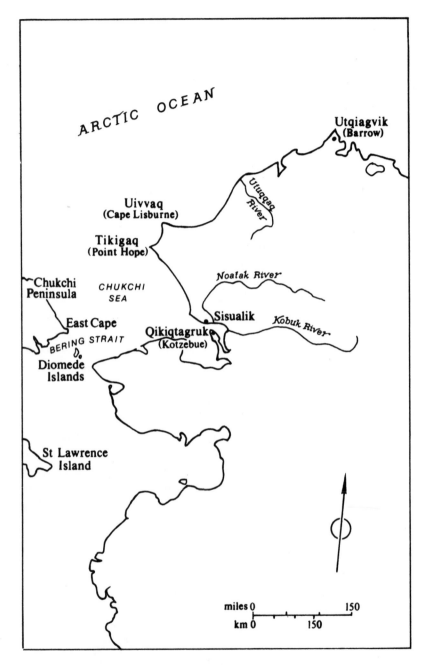

NORTHWEST ALASKA

alive and how each tale had its place within a complex system involving relationships with animals that must be killed and nature spirits who must be made kinspeople.

I was also lucky in having two other sources through which to reconstruct the old whale hunt. I had detailed notes from the distinguished archaeologist Froelich Rainey who worked with Tikigaq elders in 1940. And for three springs in the mid-1970s I was a crewman in an umialik's skinboat at the whale hunt. Most of the old whaling ritual had gone, but the hunt was still a sacred event. The final section of this book, a narrative poem of the hunt before culture contact, has its source in this experience.

The Stories, Storytellers, Prose and Verse

"Never tell one story. Always add a second. That way, the first one won't fall over," said old Tikigaq people.

The Prologue contains Tikigaq's two origin stories. The first, the land whale myth, infuses the whole book, while the companion story invokes the sun and moon spirits and is mainly relevant to Part Two. Part One takes the reader on a journey over Tikigaq peninsula, exploring the physical structure of the Point and village topography before showing how the land whale myth was understood in terms of local geography, and how the Tikigaq whale hunt echoed the creation story. It ends with a group of five stories which express how the whale comes awake in Tikigaq peninsula.

Part Two is largely about the whale cult and the hunt itself shown in the context of the annual cycle, its hunting patterns, journeys and thought systems. Within this sketch of the annual cycle the book's focus is Tikigaq's shamanistic religion, in which two great events dominate. First, the rituals of autumn; second, the spring whale hunt, which was itself meticulously ceremonialised.

There are three modes of writing in Part Two. First, there are the traditional stories which are spoken by two fictional narrators, who also discuss and explain Tikigaq lore. All the lines written for the two narrators have short beats and are justified to a left-hand margin. The idiom of their commentaries is modelled on the language of the stories themselves, and this in turn approximates the dialect that Tikigaq people use today when they speak English.

The names of the two narrators are those of my own storyteller and teacher Asatchaq (1891–1980) and his uncle Samaruna (c. 1870–1935). Raised before major European contact, Samaruna was Tikigaq's last great historian. Asatchaq inherited Samaruna's repertoire. Despite their link with historical people, the storytellers' voices are free from individual character. Storytelling was an impersonal art, often performed in twos or larger groups, voices layered responsively in cumulative mutual support. In the dialogues and shared monologues created here, uncle and nephew are collaborative equals in their exposition of local knowledge.

Tikigaq people valued and accumulated knowledge for three main reasons – magical, pragmatic and aesthetic: magical, because knowledge of the ancestors and rituals contained and expressed spiritual power; pragmatic, because knowledge was necessary for survival; aesthetic, because Tikigaq had a refined sense of beauty and fun. The lore was often rehearsed aloud by elders, in antiphonic, musing or catechismic séance between equals for the benefit of younger people.

Just as the persons behind the voices here are secondary, so their voices are also outside any dramatic context. They are focused in what they describe. The talk that accompanies their stories can thus be heard as a musing on "what we do", and perhaps even as an assertion of a reality which may no longer exist. The historical Asatchaq lived within this tension between the present and the imaginary. But a similar vantage point existed in the traditional period too, spurring the reclamation of myth-time through ritual and narrative.

To this contextual vagueness may be added the unpredictability of the storytellers' entrances. Tikigaq people walk in and out of company without feeling it necessary to explain themselves. The dialogue likewise comes and goes. The language of the narrators attempts to reproduce the plain, often repetitive, slightly didactic, sometimes a little sinister, Tikigaq storytelling medium. The stories they tell are direct translations from Inupiaq. The commentaries spoken by the storytellers are my own, but based on the lore recorded by them and their kinspeople over two generations: those born c. 1870 and 1890–1900.

The prose paragraphs of Part Two are largely expository. They attempt to sustain a sense of the year's movement and the activity of people and animals within the annual rhythm. The brevity of the paragraphs is intended to suggest the discrete nature of ritual action and to provide the impression of a linked series.

The verse takes off where rhythm and events conspire. The lines are long in that they attempt to sweep up and incorporate the interaction of people, equipment, places and animals into a movement at once simple and compound. I have indented alternate lines so as to suggest the stress of twoness: the sense that what *is* exists within the play of complementarity; that phenomena are related; that unique specificity will be added to or threatened; that the existence of a particular condition will be modified or replaced within the flow of time and action. The verse thus represents a kind of tackle, a reticulated or articulated pattern of noun/verb sequences whose effort it is to be there in the present, alive among things, at recognisable times, places and weather.

The Whale

The high Arctic ice-loving bowhead whale belongs to the Mysticete (moustached) group of baleen whales, and is the only species inhabiting the polar seas of the northern hemisphere.

Between thirty to sixty feet long in adulthood, and weighing about one ton per foot, the bowhead gets its name from the contour of its head, which is moulded by the arch of its single upper mandible. The lower jaw, with its white chin markings and scattered white bristles, is supported by two vast, curved jaw-bones. Barnacles and lice that mark other baleen whales are absent from the thick, smooth, gently furrowed, blue-black skin of adult bowheads.

Surrounding the body between the inch-thick skin and the inner tissue lies the whale's insulating fat. Ivory-white or pinky-yellow, depending on the whale's age, this fibrous blubber covers the whole body in a layer of varied thickness. The lips are virtually all blubber; the lateral flippers and tail flukes have a thinner covering. Elsewhere the blubber may be ten or twenty inches deep.

The head of the bowhead, reinforced with flesh, fat and cartilage for breaking young ice in frozen waters, accounts for a third of its body. Added to the head's weight are more than three hundred baleen feeding plates that hang from the two sides of the upper jaw. Set low between the corner of its mouth and the joints of the flippers are the bowhead's big, grey-lidded eyes. Behind and above the eyes are tiny ear-holes; within these lie enormous ear-bones – spherical, complex, and frequently filled with a soft, marbled wax. Above the eyes and blowholes, which mark the limit of the head – the skin round the two blowholes is often scarred from butting the ice – the whale's body narrows slightly into a waist. The lateral flippers emerge from this area; then the circumference swells before tapering cylindrically.

Towards the tail the body becomes quadrangular, and a top ridge runs backwards across the middle of the flukes, or tail-lobes, dividing these into the two halves of a semi-lunar whole. While the flippers are formed on a hand-like set of metacarpals, the flukes are boneless, the massive spinal vertebrae attenuating as they reach the tail's root.

There is a smaller, morphological variant to the dominant form of the bowhead, known to local people as *inutuq*. The inutuq has no pronounced bow to the head; its tail and flippers are proportionately small; and while the majority of bowheads have dark and slightly tapered bodies, the inutuq is greyish, round and barrel-like. Because the inutuq's meat is tender, the blubber thick and its bones very hard, this small, fat whale is especially prized. Most inutuqs pass Tikigaq early in the season; unlike the calves of other bowhead, their young are rarely seen.

In average years, whales spend autumn and winter in the Bering Sea pack-ice. Tikigaq people say that when the bowhead are ready to migrate groups of age- and sex-related whales gather and move north in a bunch. As ice shifts, closes and opens again, a new group forms and waits for its moment. This is said to happen three times each spring; according to locals, three "waves" or "runs" move past Tikigaq in roughly this pattern:

1	April and early May	large and small inutuqs
2	mid-May	adult non-inutuq bowhead of medium to large size (*usinuaq*, *usinuatchiaq* and *usinautchauraq*)
3	Late May, early June	large adults (*agvisugruk*) largest adults (*usinuagaaluk*) pregnant females (*ivlauligaaluk*) mothers with calves (*agvaalik**)

Ice break-up in the Bering Sea starts in March and early April when temperatures rise and the wind shifts from north-east to south or south-west. Broken and haphazard lanes of water open through the Bering Strait and run north into the Chukchi Sea. These channels trend directly past Tikigaq and up to the north Alaskan coast. But this shifting maze of lakes and alleys usually includes a single, well-defined nearshore lane of water that lies between the landfast ice and the older, thicker and unstable pack-ice. It is through this channel that the whales, with their preference for coastal waters, migrate.

Most adult bowhead travel alone, but females with a yearling and a guardian adult frequently migrate together. Small groups like these are followed every few miles by individuals within the same run, and such groups and individuals often surface in the same locations. Inupiaqs say that whales leave patches of bubbles where they have risen, thus

---

* *agviq* is the word for bowhead of no specified type.

marking a trail for the herd to follow and ensuring that bubble patches are repeated.

How the bowhead subsists in the winter is not known. There is little to eat on the northward migration, and the bellies of dead whales taken in the spring are uniformly empty. A Tikigaq umialik found a single gastropod in one; a few tiny fish and molluscs have been found in others. Bowhead migrate for one overwhelming purpose: to reach their summer feeding grounds in the Beaufort Sea of north-west Alaska, and east towards Amundsen Island at the boundary with Canada. There for four months they continuously forage, returning south along the coast of Siberia in early autumn.

The main prey of the bowhead are current-born zooplankton – euphausiids, copepods and amphipods: tiny, shrimp-like crustaceans with the high fat content on which whale blubber depends. Like other baleen whales, the bowhead feeds by swimming through plankton and gulping drafts of both food and water. As the whale's mouth extends the baleen packed on either side springs forward. Each baleen plate is edged with a fringe in which the plankton get tangled. When the whale's mouth closes the water is forced out and the tongue mops the plankton out of the fringes. This skimming and scooping accounts for most of the process. In heavy banks of plankton, groups of whales sometimes feed together, often swimming counter-clockwise a few body-lengths apart. But mud streaming from the mouths of breaching bowhead, and pebbles and molluscs sometimes found in their stomachs, suggest that whales are occasional bottom feeders.

The bowhead swim with long, deep dives interspersed with short periods at the surface. When they come up for air they exhale, inhale, and then dive shallowly several times in succession. As the bowhead rises, the head with its prominent blowhole appears first, followed by a V-shaped exhalation. This cloud of condensation is mixed with water from the grooves of the blowholes; the nostrils clap shut audibly when the blowhole submerges. The whale's roll continues as the rounded back emerges, and once the back has come up the head again submerges. The back goes down, and a few seconds later the head reappears to begin the next roll, again blowing and inhaling. Each sequence involves some fifteen ventilations. At the last breath in a series whales arch their backs, dive steeply and swim deep under water for up to twenty minutes before rising to breathe again.

The channels that make migration possible are not always open. On any one voyage the whales inevitably reach places where the pack-ice and the shorefast ice have slammed together, or where water has been newly frozen. But the bowhead has evolved to live year-round in the sea-ice. Its prominent nostrils allow it to breathe through cracks and small air-holes. Its streamlined back gives it sub-ice mobility, and whales sometimes find pockets of air between the ice and water.

In the absence of air-holes the bowhead can smash vertically through at least one foot of sea-ice. Rising slowly and exerting pressure with the top of its head, the whale lifts the ice to make holes within hummocks for later whales to use and keep open. If the ice is too thick or completely impassable, whales backtrack and circle in ponds and small channels to stop the water from freezing. They can, in an extremity, swim an hour or more beneath the sea-ice. But when they rise from long periods under the water they are slow and exhausted.

Singing as they travel, the bowhead use acoustic cues to identify thin ice and breathing places. Their calls reflected from the underwater keels of heavy formations are louder than from young, thin ice. The strength of an echo will tell them whether the ice is passable. But success will never be invariable and in heavy ice some younger whales may die of suffocation.

Tikigaq hunters are alert to the bowhead's acute hearing and sharp eyesight. Sounds such as footsteps on the shore-fast ice, or paddles striking the side of a skinboat, will alarm them. Some umialiks wait till a whale has exhaled before launching their skinboats; in this way the whale's breath drowns the keel's rub as the boat leaves the sea-ice.

For most of the spring the whales simply travel. Inutuqs enjoy loafing in calm bays where the skinboats await them. Neither inutuqs nor other bowhead sleep. But bowhead do play. They leap in the air and fall back on their sides, backs and bellies. They dive vertically and wave their flukes. They lunge and rise, as though standing in the water, and slide back in. They hang upside-down and slap their tails. They swim on their sides and beat the water with a flipper. Some whales leap, lunge, wave or slap just once before disappearing. Others circle, breach and flipper-slap fifty or a hundred times: alone, displaying to a rival male or a mateable female or, if they are calves, for joy and practice. The sound of flipper-slaps on calm days carries miles across the ice and water.

While bowhead appear not to feed on migration, they probably do mate and calve. For most of the year the adult whale is solitary, and migration provides temporary pairing opportunities. Around co-operative females, males are competitive and jostle one another. They occasionally lash out with their tail flukes, get hit back, or are slapped repeatedly; beyond this level of sexual rivalry they are non-aggressive. Sometimes a group of males mills round a single female, their long sharp penises which are otherwise coiled within the abdomen, erect. Females may copulate with more than one of them, and their sperms compete. As with other baleen whales, there seems to be some caressing and foreplay. Once coitus is imminent they roll upside-down and come belly to belly. Breaching and rolling, they move gracefully in unison. Then they grasp one another, rub flippers slowly, blow long and heavy, swim backwards and forwards, push down with their flukes and upward with their flippers, groaning softly and scraping with their bristles.

Calving probably takes place between late winter and early summer. The birth of a bowhead has never been recorded, but the closely related right whale calf is born tail-first and the mother guides it to the surface for its first breath. Sometimes the mother is attended by non-pregnant females; these may support the mother from below, raise the calf to the surface, cut the umbilical and look after the baby while the mother feeds. Most calves are probably born around April, and migrate with their mothers and perhaps a female escort. They are born large, and suck from two nipples on the mother's belly. Whale's milk is rich in fat, and calves grow quickly.

Calves are still with their mothers in April, May and June, suggesting they were born on the previous migration. Neonates swim close to their mother, often grasping the mother's flippers with their own; or they travel in a pool in the dip of her back, half swimming, half riding. As they grow bigger they play around and circle, swim to and fro, practise breaching, meander off, and then chase their mothers. In six months they are weaned. There is nothing to fear. Their only predators are men and women.

The Whale Hunt: a Sketch

The sea surrounding Tikigaq peninsula is frozen all winter. When a channel in the sea-ice opened in the spring and the bowhead whale migrated past the village, then Tikigaq hunters launched their skinboats.

For the eight months of winter six to eight hundred Tikigaq people lived crowded in their subterranean iglus. The men hunted seal in the brief winter daylight. Women, old people and children stayed home in the village. As spring approached, and the sun moved north across the hills, the pace of village life quickened. By late April there was 24-hour daylight. As the solitary and dangerous search for seal became less urgent Tikigaq buzzed with communal activity.

The community emerging from its underground iglus was not alone in the Tikigaq landscape. Even before the snow receded the squirrels had come up from hibernation. And as the sun moved daily further from the south the migrant species started arriving. When, around mid-April, the snow buntings fluttered back into the village, Tikigaq knew that the bowhead migration would soon follow.

But first to come were vast, plunging herds of white belukhas (dolphins). Tikigaq hunted the belukha when the bowhead was not running. Once the dolphins had come through the black whale was expected.

Whaling was done in crews of eight men in skinboats. The skinboat consisted of a sturdy wooden frame latticed with steam-bent wooden struts and covered each year by six to eight bearded sealskins. A skinboat was a Tikigaq family's most valuable possession; owned by men, each boat was managed by a married umialik couple. The male umialiks were the leading hunters in the village and they used the meat and skins they had accumulated since the summer to pay fellow members of their ceremonial houses (qalgis) to work in their skinboats. The umialik woman's part was separate but equal. While her husband hunted on the sea-ice, she, for the most part, stayed quietly in the village. This was ritually vital to her crew's achievement; her part in whaling ritual was so important that some local people claimed it was the women who largely ran the operation.

In contrast to the sometimes hidden role of women, men's work was visible and strenuous. Their first labour of the season was to cut a path for the skinboats from the south shore to the open water. Once a trail was ready the boat-sleds were manhauled to the ice-edge. At this stage each crew's main challenge was to manoeuvre the boat, with its delicate ribs and taut sealskin cover, to a good position. Competition for propitious places in the bays and headlands of the ice-coast lasted all season. As the crews spread the length of the shore to the cliffs at Imnat, umialiks looked for quiet water where the whales might stop to loaf and breathe. If they could harpoon a whale as it rose the crew would be saved an exhausting, often fruitless, chase in the skinboat.

The moment a crew arrived at the open water the long vigil started. Each man was dressed in special new clothes: two-layer caribou-skin parka and trousers, lined boots, mittens and eyeshades. Besides the umialik's harpoons and lances, the men brought their own gear: knives, bows, bird-spears, slings and seal-hunting tackle. For six weeks now, while the north wind kept the channel open, they would stand on the ice, intermittently hunt the smaller species, and watch for bowhead. When

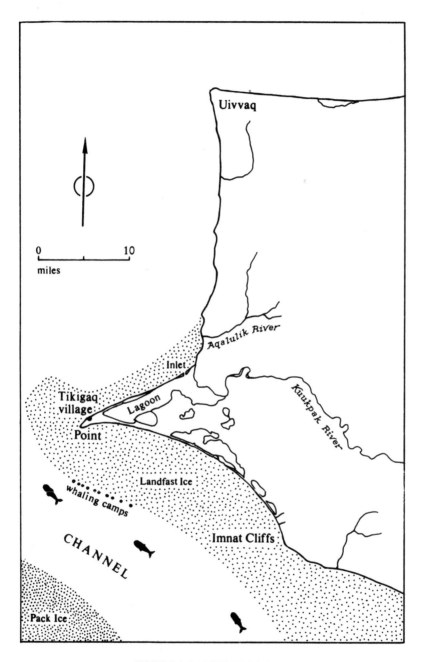

TIKIGAQ PENINSULA

the wind was from the south, the pack-ice came in, the lead closed and the hunt was suspended.

A camp place might serve a few days or a matter of minutes. The same winds and currents that made the hunt possible could always shift the ice again and force crews back to landfast ice or to travel the coast until they found fresh harbour.

The hunters ate little. Each umialik provided a large wooden bowl of frozen meat, replenished daily by a boy – nicknamed "little muskrat" – who ran between the camp and the umialik's iglu. When the whales were not running the men hunted seal, harpooned belukha and threw slings into the flocks of eider and guillemots that swept overhead to their northern breeding grounds. Cooking on the sea-ice was forbidden, so all meat taken on the hunt was pre-cooked in the village or eaten raw-frozen. The men drank from sealflipper-skins full of melted snow which hung against their bodies.

Bouts of hunting were scattered through long periods of inaction during which crews waited silently or listened to stories. The older men and shamans told the "whaling" myth of the Raven Man Tulunigraq in order magically to lure whales to them, or they hummed charm songs. If the crews made any other noise or fouled the ice – their waste was dumped well north of the whales' path – the whales would be offended and go elsewhere. The cold, monotony and hunger were exhausting. Rivals in abstinence, the men snatched sleep on the boat-sled while the rest of the crew were wakeful and vigilant. If a whale rose suddenly by the skinboat the harpooner must be ready within two or three seconds.

Most whales came less easily. When look-outs saw a whale's back or its forked plume of exhaled steam the skinboat was launched immediately and in silence. The umialik climbed in last and pushed off, steering; the seven crewmen paddled, straining through choppy water, sometimes closing in, now losing track, now watching the whale dive under ice floes, often disappearing. When the skinboat closed in on a whale the outcome lay with umialik and harpooner. As the harpooner stood up by his bench the umialik in the stern kept the angle steady. Everything depended on timing and co-ordination. The harpoon pole was heavy, the whale enormous. The harpooner aimed at a "death-place", at the heart or between cervical vertebrae. Following his strike the blade on the foreshaft disengaged. The harpooner laid his shaft in the bow. The sealskin line paid out across the gunwale; if it tangled or snagged the boat would capsize and the whale would drag it under.

The harpoon was central to all sea mammal hunting. Fitted together in five main parts there was a wooden handshaft, foreshaft, slate blade, sealskin line, and three drag-floats or buoys; these floats consisted of whole inflated sealskins. The largest of these was fitted with a mask called *inugluk* ("strange human"). Following his strike the hunter twisted and detached the handshaft; as the harpoon blade cut down and aslant in the animal's body the foreshaft uncoupled. Detached from its shaft the harpoon line ran free, dragging the floats out across the water; these slowed the whale's escape, helped drag it to the surface, marked the animal's position and buoyed it up until hunters could reach it.

Ideally a kill would be quiet and simple. But chasing a harpooned whale might last many hours and take the boat-crew miles out to sea. All this time, umialik and harpooner sang. They sang songs to lure the whale, and songs to bring the whale-floats back to them. The songs also signalled to rival umialiks that the first boat needed help. As crews arrived at the scene of the harpooning, the men planted spears and harpoons in the dying or dead animal. The boats finally linked up and towed the whale to the nearest firm ice. Here they tethered the body and the successful umialik sent a runner to the village to call his wife.

At this point the woman umialik entered a new ritual phase. "Her" whale had been taken. Dressed in new clothes, she led the wives of her crewmen to the sea-ice where she offered the dead whale water from a special pond in Tikigaq. She thanked the whale for coming and welcomed it to her family.

The senior umialiks now supervised the butchering. This must be done before the ice shifted, otherwise the whale might be lost. The first umialik to fix a harpoon took the major share. In their order of arrival, all the boat-crews had their portions. The whole whale was dismembered and hauled back to the village on sleds. Only the head was returned to sea to ensure the whale's soul's reincarnation.

When a whale had been butchered, the men spread out again and continued to hunt for as long as the ice allowed. Around the end of May, the ice became too rotten to support the boat-crews, and most of the late migrants were too heavy and fast-swimming to make hunting possible.

Back in the village, the women started to prepare for a three-day festival to celebrate the umialiks who had taken whales and to honour the souls of whales that had been killed. After the skinboats had been drawn up on the beaches and the women had prepared food, the whole village circulated through the grounds of each ceremonial house (*qalgi*). Here everyone was feasted with soured raw meat, boiled maktak, tongue, heart, liver and intestines. The whale's flukes were sliced into oval pieces, and each section distributed.

On the last day of the feast, the dancing and singing came to a climax in the skintoss game (*nalukataq*). The young men of each qalgi cut hand-grips round the edges of a walrus- or sealskin blanket. As the old men, protected from the wind by up-turned skinboats, beat their drums, umialik men and women leapt in turn on to the blanket and were tossed above the heads of the singers below them. The women, as they leapt, threw gifts of food and skins into the crowd, and the younger umaliks competed in spectacular aerial acrobatics.

By now the spring had brought new species into Tikigaq waters, and as soon the whale feast was over the community turned to seal and walrus hunting. Surplus whale meat was stored underground and left there to freeze until the autumn.

PROLOGUE

THE LAND WHALE STORY

HOW RAVEN MAN WAS MADE

Samaruna said:
First! There was an *aana*.[1]
A magical old woman.
She lived by herself.
In the dark back then.
There was no daylight.
And there was no moon.

Things were upside-down then.
People were animals.
Animals were people.
People walked on their hands.
Snow was seal oil.
Seal oil was caribou fat.

Asatchaq:
She sat in her iglu.
She sat on the sleeping bench
next to her oil lamp.
She had a grandson.

Samaruna:
People then chewed burnt oil
from their oil lamps.
They chewed it with down from their birdskin parkas.

Asatchaq:
The old woman did this.
She chewed burnt lamp oil [*puiya*].
It was black.
It turned white when she chewed it.
One day the *aana*
made a man out of puiya.

She gave it a beak
in the middle of its forehead.

The beak of a Raven.
Then she stood it on the sleeping bench,
and did nothing.

Samaruna:
Then she slept.
When the old woman woke,
the man had gone.
The *aana* looked round.
There was a young man on the floor,
with a beak in his forehead.
"Where did you come from?" said the aana.

Asatchaq:
She named all the places she could think of.
No. He didn't come from any of them.
Then she remembered
the bird's-beak man she'd made.
She said to the man,
"You must be my puiya."
"*Ii* . . . yes," the man said.
That's how Raven Man was made.
We call him Tulunigraq
because he was a Raven [*tulugaq*].

Samaruna added:
The old woman who made Raven
was the first of our shamans.

Asatchaq:
That old woman's always lived here.
She lives near the village,
but no one's ever seen her.

Samaruna:
Raven was a shaman too.
Once she'd made him,
he needed a woman.
So Raven went to find a *uiluaqtaq*:[2]
a woman who won't marry.

HOW THE WHALE BECAME LAND

Asatchaq said:
Tulunigraq lived south.
When people went to hunt,
they waited for moonlight.
They went hunting in kayaks.
When they came home,
the men met in the qalgi.

And they talked about a woman.
This woman didn't want a husband.
She was a uiluaqtaq.

Samaruna:
The uiluaqtaq wouldn't take a husband.
She killed the men who went to get her.
Killed and ate them.
When Tulunigraq heard the men talk,
he decided he would take her.
So he left the qalgi and approached her iglu.

Asatchaq:
Raven Man went to the uiluaqtaq's iglu.
But before he went in he climbed the roof.
He lifted the skylight and looked inside.
Tulunigraq saw her.
There was the uiluaqtaq.

Samaruna:
She was doing nothing.

Asatchaq:
Maybe she was combing.
Maybe sewing.

Samaruna:
Tulunigraq sang.
He sang a sleep song,
he sang to make the uiluaqtaq sleep.
Here. I'll sing it.
No . . . I've forgotten.
When Raven Man stopped, the woman lay down.
She was sleepy already.

Asatchaq:
The song had got her.

Samaruna:
When the woman laid her head down,
Tulunigraq entered.

Asatchaq:
She'd gone to the passage
to fetch a sleeping skin.

Samaruna:
Tulunigraq went in.
He came up through the entrance-hole.
But the noise didn't wake her.

Asatchaq:
I forgot.
Before he sang the sleep song,
Tulunigraq went round
looking for a piece of woman's anaq [excrement].
There are two kinds of anaq,
a man's and a woman's.
A woman's is thicker.
Raven found a piece of woman's anaq.
He thawed it in the entrance-passage.
Then he entered.

Samaruna:
Raven lay down with the uiluaqtaq.
He pushed the anaq underneath her.
She didn't wake up.
He started to feel the woman's vagina.
The uiluaqtaq went on sleeping.
Raven woke her.
"Who's this in bed with me?"shouted the woman.
She tried to push him through the *katak* [entrance-hole].

Asatchaq:
So they fought together.
Man and woman.
Then Raven Man said:
"What if I tell the men about you?
What if I tell them you shit in your sleeping skin?"

"No! don't tell them!" said the woman.
She didn't want a husband.
So Tulunigraq said he'd go and tell them.
In the end, the uiluaqtaq changed her mind.
She took the Raven.
He had tricked her.

Samaruna:
Raven was a shaman.
And the uiluaqtaq was a shaman.

Asatchaq:
Yes. She was his wife now.

Samaruna:
When they woke in the morning,
Raven went to his qalgi.
He told the men he was her husband.

Now while he sat in the qalgi,
the men told stories.
They talked about an animal,
No one could do anything.
Nobody could catch it.
So when Tulunigraq woke the next day,
he took his harpoon and his kayak,
and paddled north into the darkness.

Asatchaq:
He travelled by kayak.
Then he stopped.
Tulunigraq heard something.
An animal was breathing.
It had risen.
It was breathing.
Raven went closer.
There was something on the surface.
It stretched to the horizon.
Tulunigraq waited.
When its head rose to breathe,

Samaruna:
Nauligaa!: he struck it!
He harpooned the animal.

It dived with Raven's drag-float.
When he saw the animal had dived,
he sang to make it rise.

Uivvaluk! Uivvaluk! Uivvaluk!
Round! Round! Round!

Asatchaq:
The whale-float went round.
And the mask on the float
sang back to Raven.

Samaruna:
The animal surfaced.
The *whale* came up dry.
It rose in the water.

Asatchaq:
Dry land! *Nuna!*
It was dry land.
It was Tikigaq.

Samaruna:
Dry land from the whale.
Tulunigraq harpooned it.
When he'd done this,
he went back.
He went back to the uiluaqtaq.
And he told the people
he'd harpooned Tikigaq.

You can still see the place
where Raven harpooned it.

Asatchaq:
That's why Tikigaq's the *animal*.
The land is alive.
It's a whale he harpooned
when Raven Man married the uiluaqtaq.

Samaruna:
It's true. Raven harpooned Tikigaq.
In the summer I will show you
the wound-hole Raven made.

It's by that iglu
an old aaṅa lives in.

She's always lived there,
near the village.

When Tulunigraq struck,
the whale became land.
You can still see the wound-hole.

It's a hollow in the tundra
where the grass grows long.

In the summer I will show you.
Some old woman's always lived there.

SUN AND MOON STORY

Winter hardens and sinks deeper.
    It's mid-winter solstice. The sun goes under.
Twilight mornings thicken into darkness.
    The sun burns low, and then drops through the sea-ice.

The moon hunts now the sun is dead.
    The Moon Spirit lives in his moon-ice iglu.
Alinnaq, Moon Man, once hunted in Tikigaq.
    Alinnaq's alone. He raped his sister.

Lame Samaruna sits by the sleeping bench.
    "I'll tell another story.
I'll tell this for my nephew, Asatchaq, who asked for it."
    He named Asatchaq, his nephew.
It is evening. They have eaten. The children are sleeping.
    They lie heaped together.
Asatchaq says, "*Ki! Unipkaagin!* Tell the story, Uncle!"
    Samaruna's voice is slow and frightening.
Snow shifts across the skylight.
    The moon comes in through the frosted membrane.

Samaruna said:
Unipkaagniaqtuna: here's the other story.
It goes with Tulunigraq's.
The man's name is Alinnaq.
The man lived in Tikigaq.
He had no wife. He had a sister.
And this sister didn't have a husband.
The man's name was Alinnaq . . .
And when Alinnaq came home from hunting,
he would go to his qalgi.
But sometimes when his sister was alone in their iglu,
she saw the seal oil lamps go out.
She couldn't understand.
She didn't understand why this happened.
Alinnaq's sister didn't have a husband.

Now when the lamps went out,
she found a man had come into the iglu.
It was dark in the iglu,
and the man who came in raped her.
When the lamps went out,
a man entered and raped her.
And when she knew this man was coming,
when she knew what would happen,
Alinnaq's sister prepared for his visit.
She took her lamp,
and dipped her finger in the bottom.
There's always soot at the oil lamp bottom.
Now she was ready.
When the man was on top of her,
she would brush her fingers on his forehead.

This is what she did when he came to fuck her.
When he next came to visit,
and lay on top of her,
she brushed his forehead with her fingers.

The next evening, when Alinnaq was at his qalgi,
Alinnaq's sister left the iglu.
She went looking for a man with soot on his forehead.
She went to all the qalgis.
Alinnaq spent his evenings in the qalgi.
He always spent his evenings in the qalgi.
And Alinnaq's sister went round all the qalgis
and looked down through their skylights.
She lifted the edge of the membrane window,
and looked down through the skylight.
She was looking for the man with soot on his forehead.

And when she arrived at her brother's qalgi,
and lifted the edge of the skylight membrane,
she saw the men sitting there.
The men sitting in their qalgi.

She looked into the qalgi.
There was her brother.
The man with the soot mark was her brother.
It was her brother who had come and raped her.
Her own brother had done this to her.

She went back to her iglu.
She went home and made anaq.
She urinated in her *qugvik* [chamber pot].
And she took a knife and cut her breasts off.
When she'd cut her breasts off,
she chopped them in pieces.
Then she dropped the pieces in her qugvik,
and stirred them up with her blood and excrement.
When she'd done this, she picked up the qugvik:
She walked back to her brother's qalgi.
She went in.
Alinnaq was sitting with the qalgi men.
She came in through the katak.
She approached her brother.

She was carrying her qugvik,
and she offered him the qugvik.
She put it on the floor where Alinnaq was sitting.
And she said to her brother,
"Since you love me so much,
Here, take my breasts,
my blood, my excrement and urine.
Eat them!"
Alinnaq was silent. He did nothing.
Then he gathered his tools.

Asatchaq:
He stood up.

Samaruna:
When Alinnaq stood up,
he walked round the oil lamp.

Asatchaq:
In the sun's direction.

Samaruna:
He walked in the direction
that the sun moves.
And his sister took her qugvik,
and started to follow.
And his sister said,
"Since you love me so much,
Here, take my breasts,

Asatchaq:
"take my breasts . . .

Samaruna:
"take my blood, excrement and urine.
Eat them!"

Alinnaq walked.
He tried escaping.
But his sister followed.
And as he went round,
when Alinnaq was underneath the skylight,
he started to rise.
He rose from the floor, through the qalgi skylight.

His sister followed.
His sister rose after him.
She was carrying her qugvik.
She shouted what she'd said to him.
She left the qalgi through the skylight.

And when they reached the sky,
Alinnaq called out to her,
"*Ki!* Listen! I'm a man and you're a woman.
You don't go hunting in the winter.
You go to the sun.
I am a hunter. I'll go to the moon."

So Alinnaq's sister went to the sun.
That's why the sun is bloody at sunset.
It's the blood from her breasts.
It's from Alinnaq's sister.

Asatchaq said:
Ii . . . Yes . . . Alinnaq!
He still chases his sister.
When he catches her up,
he sleeps with her again.
My father saw it over Tikigaq.
He covered her body.
Then the sun got angry.
The moon started fighting.
And after this happened there was an earthquake.

Samaruna:
Sometimes it's the other way.
The sun gets in front and smears soot on his forehead.
Then everyone sleeps.
Like shamans in sleep trance.
Men sleep four days; women five.

Asatchaq:
Men sleep four or five days, women six.
That's what I've heard.

Samaruna:
On the sixth day there's an earthquake.
Then the people wake suddenly.
The women look for seal fat.
They put fat in the lamp flame.
Then the lamp flares up.
It makes soot on the window.
This makes the earth steady.

Asatchaq:
Then a shaman must travel.
The men in the qalgi tie his body.
The shaman crouches by the sleeping bench.
His soul goes up.
The shaman travels.

Samaruna:
He seeks Alinnaq's iglu.

Asatchaq:
He asks Alinnaq to make the earth stop shaking.

Samaruna:
Alinnaq can see our oil lamps.

Asatchaq:
And if Tikigaq hunters need more game,
if animals are scarce,
the shaman asks him to send them seals and caribou.

Samaruna:
Alinnaq's alone up there.
There's no woman to help him.

He has everything else.
But he doesn't have a woman.

Asatchaq:
Round the walls of his iglu,
run herds of caribou.
Outside, there's a tub.
Alinnaq keeps whales there.
My father saw this on a spirit journey.
He asked Alinnaq to send him a whale.
At the next new moon,
My mother raised her pot up through the sky-hole.
Alinnaq dropped a whale soul in it.
All this was so. My parents saw it.

Part One
Tikigaq: Whale

THE NAME

When in the summer you stand on Imnat cliffs and face west the eye meets a beautiful and strange landscape. From the cliff base, just above sea level, a triangle of tundra, fringed with a gravel beach, ponds and marshland, curves out through the sea, tapers into the distance and fades in a blur to the north-west. At the tip of this peninsula, just visible from the cliffs on a clear day, is Tikigaq, an Arctic village that has been occupied for two thousand years: first by societies that hunted walrus and seal, finally by a people who hunted the bowhead whale.

Up until the mid-nineteenth century the village on the Point was the centre of a numerous and far-flung society. At the height of its power over thirteen hundred people lived and travelled Tikigaq's vast coastal and inland territory, and for nine months each year the village itself supported half this population. In the winter the men hunted seal, in the spring they chased the whale. In the summer months they abandoned their underground iglus and travelled inland and up-coast to barter with other Inuit and to hunt caribou. Coming home from the south in the autumn they would often land their boats at Imnat and scale the cliffs to catch their first glimpse of the Point. As they gazed across the miles that still separated them from the village, they mused, "There's Tikigaq!"

"*Ii*! Yes! There's *nuna* [land]!"

A third might then murmur, "Yes. There's Tikigaq. There's *nigrun* [the animal]!"

Coded within these names, and especially the two nicknames, were myths and histories that were vital to Tikigaq, its story of origin and, by extension, the whale hunt. But before tracing how name, myth and whale were interconnected we must explore the implications of Tikigaq's three names.

The word Tikigaq names Tikigaq peninsula, its Point and the village on the Point. The people who live in the village and its wider territory are Tikigagmiut: "Tikigaq people", or "people who inhabit Tikigaq".

Most place names in north Alaska are quite simple descriptions of geography or hunting possibilities. Thus there are villages called "the Point", and "Almost an Island". Two others are called "Belukha Hunting Place" and "Fish-netting site". Some names allude to local folklore. For example, "Place where a boy once hunted snowy owls". The name

Tikigaq is different. The word is in two parts. The first, *tikiq*, means "index finger". The second part is archaic and obscure. But Tikiq + -aq most probably mean: "something like an index finger". The archaism of *-aq* attests to Tikigaq's antiquity, but more important here is the fusion of thing (the finger) and its function. For the land is an *index finger* only because it is extended, pointing.

Devoid of conventional connotation, the name Tikigaq is a metaphor about itself and nothing else. The finger alludes neither to topography, nor to hunting, nor to animals. Each of these may be implied, because Tikigaq peninsula *is* where the finger points; and the finger points into the sphere of whales and seals. Essentially, however, the name tells us not what the people do at Tikigaq, but what the land does. *It* points.

The beauty of the peninsula, its ambiguity and its power to suggest images have given rise to a mass of stories and folklore. A glance at the map suggests that the Point looks startlingly like a harpoon and a raven's bill. But however strongly the Point may resemble these, there is little in recorded Tikigaq tradition to suggest anything – at least on the horizontal plane – more than the pointing finger.

"Why does it point?" I asked my informants.

"It points into the sea."

"It just points," said another.

"It's a finger like this," a third responded.

His hand on the map revealed a broader pattern: the finger was not anatomically isolated but, extending from an outstretched fist, belonged to a clenched hand. The knuckles were the northern cliffs at Uivvaq. The bulge of the thumb was the Imnat headland.

"And Tikigaq village is the nail at the end of the finger!" said a voice overlaying his elderly uncle's at one of my interviews.

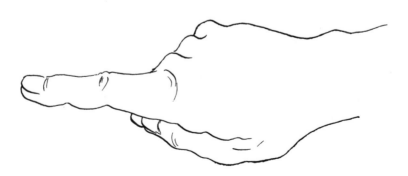

"You don't know . . ." his uncle growled. Amiq, an English-speaking Tikigaq teenager, happened not to know that the word *kukik* means both fingernail and harpoon point. Perhaps this convergence of finger and harpoon symbols predated Amiq's immediate forebears. A fragment of Raven Man's story tells that when the Raven Man had harpooned Tikigaq he tied the harpoon line to the cliffs at Uivvaq. The image here suggests that the harpoon line is the long, thin beach that stretches from the Point towards the northern mainland. This line is attached perhaps both to Raven Man's harpoon point and to the Tikigaq "land whale". Flung far into the sea by the harpoon line of its gravel beaches, the blade of the Point plunges deep into the whales' and seals' path. Like the hunters who take off from the Point to harpoon animals, Tikigaq harpoons the ocean.

Speculative as this may be, the images of finger and harpoon have points of convergence. The finger has a nail (*kukik*) and belongs to a system of joints, bones and ligaments. The harpoon, likewise, is a composite. Its point (*kukik*) extends from articulated parts. Jointed and ligatured, it has forward extension. But, again, more important is the energy that Inuit see in composite beings. And Tikigaq's two nicknames suggest that the life implied by the pointing finger is embodied in a dramatically larger symbol.

While the index finger extends horizontally, Tikigaq's nicknames point vertically inward, to the earth's own nature and to Tikigaq's myth-time.

The primary meaning of *nuna* is "land", non-sea, and the inland territory. As a name, however, nuna evokes the fresh-made earth of myth, when Tikigaq rose from primal waters.

"Tikigaq nuna," an old man told me, "isn't real land. At the moment of creation, the land was something else: the animal."

This is *nigrun*, the animal that was, and which still becomes, nuna.

Nigrun, the sea beast that Raven Man lured with his whaling song, was harpooned, rose and died to become nuna. This land, this animal, was Tikigaq Point and its peninsula.

But the mythic process is never complete. The land whale myth takes place "back then" (*taimmani*), but *back then* time, so long as people go on telling stories, is also present and continuous. Myth events are real. "The stories," storytellers never tired of saying, "are true!" Acts of creation survive in stories. But to keep this life going each generation must repeat the stories and enact them in rituals. The same theory underlies the life of Tikigaq. The presence of the land whale lasts just as long as its soul life is supported.

Soul, Name as Soul, and Soul in Tikigaq

The souls of people, and some animals, were, like so much in the Tikigaq cosmos, multiple and composite. Tikigaq people believed there were three human souls. One soul, the "life force", was mortal and vanished at death. The "soul of personality", on the other hand, moved "somewhere to the east, where the light comes from", or hung around the village, perhaps to become a shaman's helping spirit. The third soul lay in name. Put another way, a person's name *was* soul; without name, or several names, no one was properly alive.

The transmission of name-soul worked as follows. An old woman, for instance, died, and her newborn grandchild inherited her name; in doing so she became her grandmother (*aana*). This transfer of soul was automatic. The parents called their own child "*aana*". At this second grandmother's death the name would go to another relative, and so the soul was reborn until the family line lapsed.

Land, of course, neither lives nor dies in this way. It has no soul to bestow or inherit. But Tikigaq, the animal, had supernatural character. The moment of its birth was enshrined in the whale myth. This birth coincided with the death of the animal. The animal was dead, but its name, and the soul within it, continued.

To outline how this presence was embodied in the Point we must explore the geography and architecture of Tikigaq. Once this is done the soul of the animal (*inua*) must be added to the three we have examined.

THE LAND GROWS AND DIES

From the air and from the cliffs the Point and its beaches appear vulnerable and fragile. But like many sand spits on the shallow Alaskan Arctic coast Tikigaq has ancient geological history.

What sets Tikigaq apart is its scale and elegance. Sweeping west from the cliff-base, the Point seems in motion. It has life; it has purpose; it has magical suggestion.

"Tikigaq nuna isn't real land," the old man repeated.

"What is real land?"

"Inland, up there," the old man murmured, drawing his hand across the hills where the sun was hanging.

Real land is mainland. The frail-looking arm of the Tikigaq spit is fragmented, virtually an island, flung-out in the ocean; a composite of beaches, ridges, ponds, marsh, tundra. Viewed from the cliff-top, wrinkled in the atmosphere, the Point lies on the western horizon: motionless, dynamic; finger, sea beast and harpooned animal . . . "Like two whale jaws laid there!" a young man once suggested as we stood on Imnat.

Maps, Time: Horizontal, Vertical

In 1892, a year after he arrived in Tikigaq, the missionary John Driggs made an influential convert. This was the shaman Anaqulutuq, a shaman, a great dancer and, that rare thing for Inuit, completely bald-headed. Anaqulutuq was also a draughtsman, and for Dr Driggs, he drew the outline map shown here.

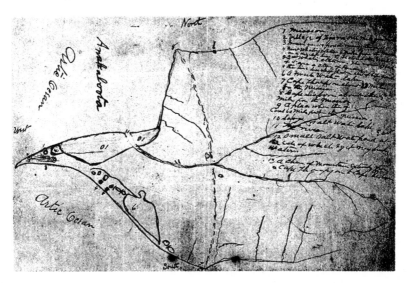

SHAMAN'S MAP

Like all Tikigaq men the shaman was a hunter. To hunt is to travel; and to travel is to measure distances and calculate trajectories of motion over moving surfaces. Travel in the Arctic, where the ice, light and wind conditions are in constant change, depends on a super-sharp awareness of surrounding space and comprehension of the interplay of force and angle. Thus the faculty that could calculate the direction of a harpoon strike from shifting ice at a seal moving against the current in the twilight in a cross-wind could, with little mental hardship, construct for itself mental maps of varied and complex geographic features. The Inupiaq grasp of encircling space and the broad Arctic geography is wonderfully expressed in the following story of intercontinental travel:

Asatchaq said:
Migalliq was a Tikigaq hunter.
It was winter.
He went hunting for seal, and the sea-ice broke.
When he knew he was adrift, Migalliq kept walking.
He used the stars to guide him.
As he walked, Migalliq noticed three different currents.
A fast current ran north.
The second carried slush-ice south.
A third, further out, was also fast.
The fast north-moving current
threw fish on to the slush-ice.
Migalliq gathered fish, and went on walking.

Time passed, and he saw land.
Migalliq guessed he was coming to Siberia.
He continued walking,
and when he reached shore, some people met him.
They took him home with them.
He'd landed in Siberia.

So they took him in.
They didn't kill him.
And in the spring, when it was time for whaling,
Migalliq went with them.
But when the first whale came through,
they let it go by.
Migalliq wondered why they didn't chase it.
"The first whale is taboo," the people told him.

Soon another came through.
It was a grey whale.
They harpooned it.
The grey whale has good meat,
short white baleen and thin *maktak* [skin and blubber].

Migalliq spent the winter there.
And next spring he decided to teach them
how to hunt the bowhead.

The people agreed.
And when a bowhead whale came through,
Migalliq harpooned it.
The Siberians liked this kind of whale.
They started to hunt it.
They learned from a Tikigaq man.

But the harpoon heads the Siberians used were made of copper.
Their copper was scarce.
They only had a little.
Migalliq told them to use slate.
They should get this instead of copper.

When the sea froze next winter,
Migalliq said he was going home.
He told the people, and they helped him get ready.
When he was ready,
they took Migalliq to the qalgi.

And there in the qalgi, on his back,
the women tattooed a map of their coastline.
They tattooed an outline of Siberia.
They did this so everyone in Tikigaq
would believe Migalliq's story.

Before he left,
Migalliq told the people he had stayed with:
"When summer comes, you must come to our side,
and fetch slate for harpoon points.
I'll be waiting at Uluurat."
He told them where this was.
At Imnat, south of Tikigaq.
At the cliffs, by Isuk.

Migalliq left. He walked back to Tikigaq.
And when he arrived, he found his wife.
He told her where he'd been,
but she didn't believe him.

So Migalliq said,
"Call the people to the qalgi."
Everyone came.
And when they were inside,
Migalliq took his parka off.

He showed them his back.
They saw the coastline
tattooed on his back.
This made them believe him.

Now when it was summer,
and whaling was over,
Migalliq went south to the cliffs.
He waited at Uluurat.
And when he'd waited for a while,
a skinboat appeared.
It had come from Siberia.
Only the family he had stayed with came.
They'd brought him copper from Siberia,
and they gave Migalliq copper in exchange for slate.
When they'd taken all they needed, they returned to Siberia
before Tikigaq people came and found them.

This story's explosive interest to a local audience must be passed over here.[1] Perhaps most astounding to a twentieth-century reader is that both parties should know each other's coastline, in part by hearsay, and in minute detail. The tattooed map on Migalliq's back is astonishing enough. Equally extraordinary is the Siberians' landfall, achieved on an alien continent, an enemy coastline, at an outcrop in the cliffs no more than fifty yards long.

Not everyone had the luck and guile of the travellers in this story. But along with essential geographic knowledge all Tikigaq people acquired a sense of the vertical dimension. A traveller's knowledge was incomplete without a sense of former time and previous selves. Tikigaq children routinely learned that the individual's presence was simply an element in a long continuity. The traveller's own moment of life stretched back and spread far. How far this back-time of story and knowledge might go was illustrated by a comment made to me by Umigluk in 1980: "This side [Alaska] and the far side [Siberia] were once a single land. Our rocks were their rocks. That was before the sea divided us. That's what my father told me, and his father told him."

So far as I understood him, Umigluk (born in 1900) was alluding to the Bering land bridge that joined the old and new worlds until the glaciers withdrew fifteen thousand years ago.

Prehistory and Earth-changes

The Tikigaq peninsula has an ancient geological history. Around 70,000 BC, as the first diagram suggests, the shape of the peninsula was roughly as it is today. The second diagram shows what happened about twelve thousand years ago when the sea withdrew in the final glaciation, leaving the sea-bed to become tundra. When the glaciers waned about six thousand years later the sea rose again and Tikigaq reverted to the shape it has held, with minor changes, to the present.

The creative and destructive process did not stop when the glaciers retreated but continued, on a smaller scale, for the next few thousand years. Much of this action, as the Inuit witness, is annually repeated in the continual disintegration of the sandstone and mudstone walls of the Imnat cliffs, to which the Point owes its existence. The rock that loads the beach at each spring thaw is swept into the sea after break-up and pounded into stones and gravel. Each summer when the ice has gone the current drags gravel out to Tikigaq, where thousands of tons are heaped by the surf on the south beach until autumn freeze-up. The extent to which the south shore grows may be appreciated in relation to Tikigaq's ancient Ipiutak site. The Ipiutak were a pre-Inuit people who colonised the spit about AD 1 and vanished about five hundred years later. The Ipiutak village lay on the south side of the Point so as to give hunters quick access to seal and walrus. As the Point built from the south, the remains of Ipiutak "moved" north. Today the last Ipiutak ruins are being cut away on the north side, presently about a mile from the (new) south shore where they originally lay.

Using the present position of Ipiutak as one measure it has been calculated that the Point grows, from the south side, by approximately eighty yards each century. The growth of the Point is visible in the beach ridges that stretch across it from east to west. The newest ridges start on the south side as barren gravel humps; as new ridges form, and the older humps move north, grasses and other tundra plants take root in them; by the time a ridge has reached the northern edge of the Point its frozen interior of gravel will have been overlaid with turf. The Inuit people who colonised the Point after the disappearance of Ipiutak built their underground driftwood and whalebone iglus into these hummocks on the north side.

This growth of the Point from the south represents only one side of the story. Complementing the build-up on the south shore, silt from the Kuukpak River that enters the sea north of Tikigaq forces its way back on to the shore to consolidate the thick north-side turf.

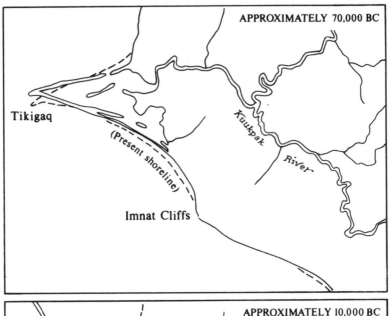

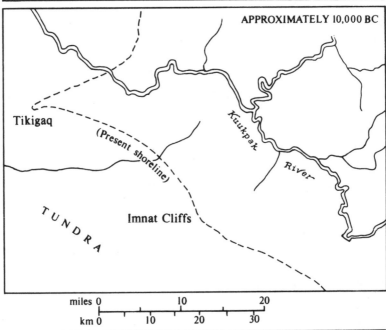

Countering this build-up on both shores there is also a process of erosion which stops the Point from growing. Erosion occurs in the summer and autumn when the bluffs on the north beach are ripped out by surf. Dr Driggs, the first Tikigaq missionary, reckoned 185 feet of land were torn away in the eighteen years that followed his arrival in the summer of 1890. The process has accelerated. In the summer of 1977 I walked along Tikigaq's north side with Tigluk to inspect the previous season's damage and identify iglu ruins. The ruins which now formed part of the shoreline were "in the middle of the Point' when Tigluk was growing up in the 1920s. Tigluk told this story:

> Long ago when a man sat fishing on the north side, and his wife crossed the Point to bring him meat, she used to take a pair of extra boot soles with her for the return trip. The Point was so wide in those days that your boots wore out from just walking across it.

The whimsical exaggeration in this folk-tale reflects both half-truth and anxiety. For example, a storm in October 1893 submerged the Point in three feet of water, flooding iglus and qalgis and forcing the community to shelter on high ground east of the village.

As the world "grows old", say other tales, and moves further from the state of perfection in which ancestors knew it, so the land decays. One story evokes the time "not long ago, when the Point was so huge and had so many iglus that people got lost and couldn't find their houses". Though these stories evoke dreams of a more substantial past they are also expressions of keen observation. The shape of the Point has remained more or less constant, but in size, over the last two hundred years, it has been shrinking. The Tikigaq population likewise saw a sharp fall in the mid-nineteenth century, even before contact with white man's diseases.

The observation of the Tikigaq people converged on an overwhelming notion: the Point was alive. Like an animate being, it grew and died; earth, like people, had myth-life that extended to the present. Again, like its keepers, who must preserve ritual purity for their hunting to succeed, the Point must be kept pure. Animals, especially whales, would avoid polluted land. Herein lay Tikigaq's responsibility. So long as each generation observed taboos and rituals established by ancestral shamans and whalers the Point would cohere. Moving against this, however, was the irreversible decline of each generation as it receded from the archaic ideal. The shrinkage of Tikigaq was thus taken for granted.

The Point also suffered omens and disasters. When, for example, the wind makes the pack-ice ram the shore, the whole Point shakes. And Tikigaq had earthquakes, attributed, as the Sun and Moon myth shows, to solar eclipses, which themselves are the result of human folly. The earth must be husbanded, and earthquakes contained by human intervention. The last big quake happened in the early nineteenth century, and disaster was averted only when a shaman hopped across the Point and, as Asatchaq told me, "pulled the land together":

> The one-legged shaman Talaviliiraq went up on the first ridge on the south side, jumping on his one leg. All the people were in their iglus. Cracks opened in the ground all over the village, and the water rose through them . . . Talaviliiraq came from the southernmost ridge. When he got to a crack he jumped over it. The cracks in the earth smoked like open water in the sea-ice. That shaman was well paid for what he was doing. Before this, there had been an eclipse. The earthquake came four or five days later. Only one place never moved. There was an iglu built on the place where Tulunigraq harpooned the land. When the earthquake came, this house never moved.

Thus the Point grew and died; the earth shook and fell away; when earthquakes happened, water appeared "as if between ice-floes"; sometimes the sea engulfed the village, but then drained off quickly. Each of these events evoked the life of earth and a history of that life. This process of change, in myth and local history, is recorded, as we'll see, by collective memory.

IGLUS, QALGIS AND CYCLIC CHANGE

While Ipiutak had faced south, Tikigaq was built on the north side. This was slightly inconvenient, because the richest hunting grounds lie south of the Point. But for the purpose of excavating large, deep iglus the northern ridges offered the best building space.

For the thousand years before this century Tikigaq built with driftwood logs, whalebone and turf. Like all Inuit iglus Tikigaq houses were in two main parts, with an entrance-tunnel (*qanitchaq*) leading from outside into the living area. The living room was a rough log cabin with a plank floor, membrane skylight and a small ventilation hole, while the entrance-passage consisted almost entirely of whalebone: mostly ribs, jaws, vertebrae and scapula. These were articulated into a passageway, the height and length of which varied according to the builder's status as a whale hunter.

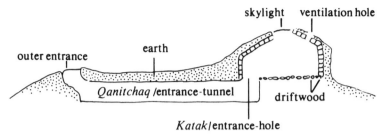

Tikigaq *iglu*: cross section

The entrance-passage served a number of purposes. It operated as a storm shed and cold trap, isolating the living room from the wind and cold. Since it was unheated and unlit the passage also served as a storage cellar for meat and equipment; larger iglu passages might have alcoves for cooking and sleeping cut into the side, but these were used sparingly. As stories attest, the dark, unheated passage was an ambiguous, semi-domesticated space in which frightening supernatural events were said to happen.

Just as the passage represented a transition between the upper village and the iglu living room, so there was a second transitional area. This was the entrance-hole (*katak*, from the verb katak, "to fall") which led vertically from the passage to the iglu chamber. Local stories likewise represent this circular hole as a locus of magical, transformative activity.

The ceremonial houses (qalgis) were built in the same way as iglus, only they were much larger; and while the iglu had a single sleeping platform benches were set round at least three of the qalgi walls. Because whaling rituals took place in the qalgi, and whale hunt crews were organised from there, the main room of each house had two bowhead jaws mounted in the walls or the ceiling. Umialiks thus sat, danced, sang and exchanged gifts within whale jaws that the founding qalgi owners had built around them.

Tikigaq iglus were almost always built with south-facing passages, and variations on this were expressed in house names like "cross-wise" or "with its end towards the land". Many large, extended families lived in clusters of iglus with interconnecting passages. These "clan" groups defined various parts of the village in terms of small family demesnes. Tikigaq's ceremonial houses – there were six in the early nineteenth century; some old people claim there were once twelve – had all collapsed by 1910, but it is likely that each had its place (now impossible to plot) within a particular "clan" area, each of which was dominated by the most powerful umialiks.

Most of the features described so far were invisible on the surface. In the winter the rounded, sod-covered chambers of the iglus with their tapering passages blended with the shifting snow dunes; in the summer they rose from the contours of the ridges to which they often gave scarcely differentiated emphasis. The village was much more strikingly manifested by what stood above ground. As Beechey, the British mariner who gave Tikigaq its English name, Point Hope, remarked in 1826, the Point was covered with "a forest of stakes driven into the ground". This forest consisted of meat racks, burial and boat-frame platforms and dog-tethering stakes. Most impressive were the whale-jaw arches and the tripods of lashed whale ribs that stood in the grounds surrounding each qalgi.[2]

The clutter round the iglus was immense and extraordinary. Inside, women kept house with orderly and strict method. Beyond the iglu chamber, the village was alive with the materials of work and the detritus of manufacture. Just as the Point itself was made and unmade while the north and south shores grew and fell away, so the village was littered with the bones of animals which had come through the village's dietary and technological system in a continuous process of recycling and discard.

Hauled back to the spit each year to feed and clothe its busy inhabitants were thousands of animals and birds: whale, seal, walrus, polar bear, belukha, caribou, wolverine, marmot, wolf, geese, loons, golden eagle, peregrine, to name only the larger species. While their meat was consumed or stored underground in the permafrost of iglu ruins, which served as caches, their skins, sinew, ivory, antlers and bones were re-articulated into hunting and travelling equipment, carved into ceremonial gear or thrown out to disperse through the village and eventually sink into the tundra or find their way to the sea. The remains of dead Tikigaq people, whose bodies were laid out with their equipment on racks or in shallow graves from which they rose to the surface, likewise kept company with the living and were scattered through the village with the bones of animals which had been eaten over the generations. To walk through Tikigaq was thus always to encounter past hunting and ancestors' relics. Death, underfoot, was the physical presence of occiputs, jaw-bones, clavicles and femurs. Even today it is no more rare to kick up the vertebra of some long-dead forebear than it is to stumble, in the south shore grasses, on the bones of seal, walrus and belukha that were butchered last season.

The north shore offers a more historically detailed spectacle. Here the low bluffs are composed of iglu ruins. When, each summer, the sea erodes a new section of nuna, fresh strata of ancestral houses are revealed to the present. The crumbling sides of the beach-head bristle with the signs of meals eaten and with household and hunting equipment: seal ribs, birds' wings, dog skulls, needles, skin-scrapers, spear and arrow points, shamans' dolls and children's toys, fragments of drums and masks and amulets. All this the sea makes off with, only to toss it back along the shore a few seasons later. Tikigaq hunters are keen antiquarians. They live cheerfully with relics and cherish the curiosities they bring back from their journeys. All they discover is eventually dispersed in further cycles – as they know they themselves, and the things they have made, will be dispersed in coming generations.

TIME AND STORIES: PLAYING OUT MYTH

Tikigaq's main sacred sites were on the Point, but residues of ancient life lay everywhere. Old iglus, graves and abandoned camp sites marked the tundra, beaches, hills and riverbanks with history.

"Big old Nigliq died at Tapkagruq. Don't forget to visit his iglu when you land there!"

"Your uncle Pauluagana killed a stranger on that hillside. This is the song he composed about it."

"When we go to the river, you will see where your grandmother stopped the north wind blowing."

"Don't sleep near those rocks! The *iraaq* [baby ghost] will attack you!"

Each generation hunted the same animals. The places themselves stayed as ancestors had known them. But where the ancestors had fought or died, seen visions or shamanised, they left knots, whorls, vortices of human implication on the landscape. To be in a place of death or vision was to relive the story and extend its relationship with the present.

When the six-year-old Asatchaq visited the ruined cliffs at Irinniq he had just this experience. It was summer 1897; Asatchaq had come north with his family and a group of other skinboat travellers. Gigantic rock piles, fallen from the cliff-face many generations previously, blocked the beach and towered from the water. As they approached in the clatter of the guillemots whose eggs they had come to gather the men in the boat told Irinniq's story. An ancestor history; an avoidable disaster. "The women broke taboo; they brought the cliffs down!" Eighty years later, in Asatchaq's telling, childhood memory is woven in with the old men's story:

While the men [in the history] were on the cliffs, the women were
in their tents sewing.

And when *we* went there, I was in my uncle Isigraqtuaq's
skinboat. This was the first time I travelled north. Natchigun
and his wife were with us. And Natchigun told us about Irinniq.
We left Tikigaq while there was still sea-ice. As we travelled,
Natchigun told us how the rocks had fallen.

We came ashore near Irinniq, and the men went up the cliffs
for eggs. I was scared of climbing; I am not a climber. So I made
my aunt Tarruq hold my hand as we went up. And I seemed to
be slipping, even though I was holding someone . . . *irrigii!*
[exclamation of fear].

And while the men went up the cliffs, Natchigun and Tikiq told
the women how the rocks had fallen.

The men [in the story] told their wives not to sew while
they were climbing. But someone didn't listen. The women and
children were buried when the cliffs fell down on them. When
they returned the men could hear their cries beneath the rocks.
But they couldn't help them.

So when the men [in our party] began climbing, Natchigun
and Tikiq told us what had happened to those people. The men
had warned the women not to sew. But they did, and the cliff fell.

Tikigaq stories were divided into two classes. There were myths and
legends; and there were ancestor histories, like Irinniq's story. Myths
and legends took place in a world half formed, when humans and animals
shared identities and the cosmos was dominated by tricksters like the
Raven Man and Alinnaq. Ancestor histories outlined the lives of recent
people, described how village feuds began, and recalled Tikigaq's main
shamans and umialiks over five past generations. Beyond that backward
limit history merged with legend, and the lines of connection with the
living vanished.

Whichever class they belonged to, all stories were received as *true*.
While myth was the metaphysical backdrop against which the ancestors
were seen to move, each present generation pursued its existence within
a sphere simultaneously inhabited by both. Tikigaq's experience of time
was therefore both organised and contradictory. On the one hand the
histories were recorded with intense regard for accuracy. On the other,
events in archaic time, about which people often had discordant versions,
were perceived to have equal validity in fact. The time-strata co-existed.
Shamans, in their dreams and visions, entered ancient story realms and

returned to reinforce collective experience of the archaic realities. Thus time was at once divisible, uniform and recurrent.

The story of the Raven, the end of "upside-down time" and the death of the sea beast all happened in myth-time, "back then", taimmani. And while Tikigaq's creation lay in the vague, archaic sphere that other legends shared, the primal harpooning marked the beginning of Tikigaq's history. The truth of the harpooning was never questioned. It provided the basis for present existence. The Point, with its wound, was *there*. The evidence lay underfoot.

Within this view lay another discord. On the one hand people understood themselves to be reborn ancestors whose names and characters they inherited by reincarnation; on the other, they felt they were poor copies of these ideal past figures. In a sense this idealist view was pragmatically based. The ancients had evolved a way of life that was *proved* by the fact of the community's survival. Thus while present people "reproduced" their forebears, the forebears had successfully completed their lives, while the living continued their uncertain struggle.

The stories of oral tradition provided models for a host of different skills and modes of being, and the narrative repertory was recited each year at the start of the annual qalgi rituals. Thus each autumn a vast company of ancestors "returned" to the village. Shamans, great umialiks, dancers, warriors and adepts at sea-ice survival were evoked, and their genealogies explained by the elders.

Looming from the mass of storied heroes, Raven Man and the uiluaq-taq held a dominant place in the narrative culture. While Tikigaq's harpooning happened in the vague depths of myth-time, the story's sequence of events was crucial to the present. Because Raven Man took the uiluaqtaq before encountering the sea-beast, the uiluaqtaq's presence was implied in the harpooning. Without the wife's mystical collaboration the animal's death would have been impossible. The two great male and female hunters were thus both Tikigaq's parents and the first umialiks. The primal couple and their land whale became a three-member "family".

One important aspect of the earth corresponded with Raven-and-his-wife's nature. All was in twos. Tulunigraq was bird and human; the uiluaqtaq was both a destroyer and a life-giving partner; the married couple was a group of two. Nuna, likewise, had a dual character: empirically it was earth; mythologically it was animal. And earth had a further twofold nature. Just as the harpooner was associated with the sea and his iglu-dwelling wife was identified with land, so nuna combined the properties of earth and sea, and also, by the same association, of male and female character.

The dual nature of the mythic couple and the doubleness of the earth they "created" extended further than myth. As we shall see the "opposites" of earth/whale, land/sea, male/female were vital and almost endlessly evoked symbolic forces to Tikigaq people. True, on the one hand the symbols of Tulunigraq's story were embedded in a static, ancient myth. But this myth had spectacular rebirth in Tikigaq's annual experience. Just as Tulunigraq harpooned the sea-beast, so Tikigaq hunted bowhead whales. These whales migrated past Tikigaq each spring; they were part of its waters. Tikigaq nuna had emerged from these same waters. Just as Tikigaq's "parents" prefigured the umialiks, so the whales were "descendants" of the mythic land whale. The whale hunt and the myth of the harpooning thus coincided in their major details.

But Tikigaq hunters took the coincidence of myth and subsistence a large step further. Where the central acts in the myth and in whaling coincided, Tikigaq elaborated on the mythic structure of their whale hunt by re-enacting Tulunigraq's narrative and adopting the creation story's myth roles and characters. Thus, in the hunt and in certain rituals, the male umialik became Raven Man. Yet more strikingly, the uiluaqtaq was enacted by umialik women. Most stirringly of all, the third member of the "family" sometimes came to life at whaling season. This third was Tikigaq: the land whale, "animal", whose death in myth-time had made Tikigaq possible. All this was expressed in a series of stories and rituals. The rest of this section explores how each member of the primal whaling trio was evoked in Tikigaq.

MYTH ROLES

The Umialik Husband

The male umialik's myth role was straightforward. In a ritual that is described in more detail in Part Two of this book, umialik men visited a pond near the village each autumn where, according to legend, a magical whale had once been created. This whale was made by a shaman from the bloodstained parka of his raped uiluaqtaq daughter. Wearing ravenskin capes, the umialiks from each qalgi visited the whale pond in the middle of the autumn rituals and chopped discs of freshwater ice for later use in whaling ceremonials. Then, still wearing their bird capes, they returned to their qalgis, where the skins were kept all winter and then stowed in the skinboat. Some umialiks kept a ravenskin about them for the whole of the whale hunt; most reserved theirs until success was certain, when, once the crew had made a final strike and the whale was floating dead by his skinboat, the umialik thrust the raven's head into the whale's mouth or into the harpoon wound "to feed it fresh meat". Once the raven had been fed the umialik flung the skin round his neck, the bird's bill topping his head and its wings extended.

There were two gestures here: one repeated the harpooning of Tikigaq; the other reproduced Tulunigraq's identity. Just as Raven Man harpooned the sea beast, so the umialik became Raven when he took a whale. And just as the crone made a man-with-a-bird's-bill inua, so the umialik in his mask-cape took on the inua's double nature: man and raven.

The Umialik Wife

The umialik woman's myth role was more complex than her husband's and her uiluaqtaq character must be understood within a group of other symbolic positions.

In contrast to her "Raven" husband's freedom on the sea, the woman umialik stayed at home in her iglu and did nothing for most of the whale hunt. This, in essence, was her mythic role. Secluded and overtly idle like the uiluaqtaq of the story, the umialik woman was completely passive. The woman umialik, in fact, did less than her mythic prototype. While the uiluaqtaq sewed or combed and thereby committed supernatural murders (see note 2, p. 156), the umialik specifically reversed this behaviour; combing and sewing were forbidden while her husband hunted. Within this inertia lay shamanistic power. How this functioned may be seen in the umialik's parallel actions.

The woman's springtime rituals in fact started on the sea-ice. On the first day of the hunt, when the male crew left Tikigaq, the woman walked ahead to the open water. With the help of the woman the crew would have found a good place to wait, and the woman lay down on the ice with her head pointing towards Tikigaq while the men embarked and pushed off from the ice. After travelling a short distance the steersman brought the boat round and returned to the ice-edge. Silently, the harpooner leaned over the prow, dipped his weapon in the water opposite the woman and then touched her parka. When she had been "struck", the woman got up and, without looking back, walked home.

The moment she reached her iglu the woman ceased activity, and for the rest of the hunt sat passively on the sleeping bench. If she scrubbed the floor she would make the skin of the whale thin; if she used a knife her husband's harpoon line would break. To the combing and sewing taboo, sexual abstinence was added.

While her posture on the ice had resembled the rising whale and the position of her head indicated the direction from which the whale must come, woman had been the whale's body. In her ritual tranquillity she now enacted the whale's soul. Not only did she transmit to the whales the generous passivity that whales were supposed to feel towards their hunters, but she *was* already the whale's soul, resident within her Tikigaq iglu, suspended between the conditions of life and death that the hunt counterpoised and made sacred.

THE LAND WHALE

The third actor in the annual mythic drama was the whale itself. Just as Raven Man had the double character of bird and human, and the uiluaqtaq was a double creative/destructive presence, so the whale was perceived in terms of two main elements: animal and land. In the historical whale hunt these two components were brought together in a further symbol: the iglu. These images of whale, land and iglu converged in a number of Tikigaq stories. Five of these follow.

THE RAVEN AND THE WHALE

A Raven, out at sea and in search of land, finds a whale and flies through its jaws. Inside Raven finds a brightly lit iglu; a young woman on the sleeping bench tends a lamp. The woman greets the Raven but warns him not to touch her lamp. Now and then the woman disappears and then returns. Raven asks her why she is so restless. "Life," she answers, "life and breathing." The next time the woman leaves Raven goes out and the young woman falls dead into the iglu.

In the darkness the Raven starts to suffocate and lose his feathers. The young woman was the whale's soul. She had left the iglu each time the whale breathed. The lamp was the whale's heart.

Raven eventually escapes and floats with the whale and feeds on its skin. When a skinboat paddles near Raven transforms himself

into a man and cries out to the crew, "I killed the whale!" Thus he
became a great man among the people.[3]

This text is a version of Tulunigraq's story. Here as there Raven breaks
in on an isolated woman and violates her. In the Tulunigraq story this
involves trickery and rape and is followed by the death of the sea-beast.
Here, woman and animal are one and the same victim. Both stories
involve women in the death of the animal. In Tulunigraq the land-locked
uiluaqtaq contributes her power to Raven Man's harpooning. In the
present story the woman is herself the whale soul. Like the uiluaqtaq she
lives in an iglu. But the iglu here is inside a whale. The whale *is* her iglu.

Two ideas we have seen separately are now brought together. The
Tikigaq Point is an animal; umialik women enact both whale and whale
soul. And this second Raven story introduces a third idea: that the
woman's iglu *is* a whale. The physical structure of the Tikigaq iglu, with
its whalebone passage, now enters the picture.

The Iglu and Tupitkaq

Tikigaq shamans often gathered the parts of dead animals and birds and
used them for sorcery. From these bones, skins and sinews the shamans
assembled fantastic creatures, breathed life into them with songs, and
sent them on missions. This was what the father did when he made a
whale from his uiluaqtaq daughter's bloodstained parka. The practice
was called *tupitkaq*.

The whalebones forming half the Tikigaq iglu represented a ready-
made tupitkaq. In its secular and daily aspect the iglu was simply a
domestic dwelling. But especially at whaling the iglu came alive, and
brought forth life. Through the passage and the katak whales emerged
through the dry land of the Point. The midwives bringing these whales
through the katak, the "spirits" that animated the iglu, were umialik
women.

The process by which whales became whale-bearing iglus was cyclical.
First the bones of hunted whales were reassembled to become iglu
passages. Iglus were enlivened by women who had themselves "died"
on the ice, returning to animate their "dead whale iglus". From there
they lured the living, harpooned whale both to die and to join Tikigaq
land and society. This process brought fresh life to the village. When
the whale was dead its meat was brought home to be stored in the earth
of ruined iglus. With the dead whale's soul going south on its incarnation
journey the earth of Tikigaq's north side was packed with whale meat,

skin and blubber. Both in symbol and in substance Tikigaq Point was reincarnated.

The Entrance-passage and the Katak

In addition to the whalebones of the passage, the round hole (katak) leading from the passage to the living room was vital to its magical identity. Tikigaq stories often portray both the passage and katak as areas of birth, death, danger and initiation. In one tale shamans fix mobile sharpened whale jaws to the katak, through which, in deadly competition, the two men leap until one of them is cut to pieces. A travelling shaman escapes a woman with a toothed vagina only to be threatened, as he rushes to leave, by her palpitating iglu entrance passage. A child lures a drowned man back from the sea-bed through the qalgi katak. A nineteenth-century shaman "drowns" a rival's effigy in his iglu katak. Next spring the murder is repeated at sea and the victim is dragged under by a harpooned whale.

Just as stories dramatised the play of birth and death in the katak, so entry and exit were subjects of metaphysical suggestion. A father traps his son in an iglu and challenges him (impossibly) to escape underground through the permafrost; a shaman appears (impossibly) in the passage every time the girl he's chasing enters to hide. A group of shaman spirits attack a woman through the ventilation hole of her iglu. A girl and her brother keep an eagleskin hanging in the passage; when either of them dons her eagle parka they can fly off and bring home whales in their talons. A shaman dives headfirst into the passage; in transit through the katak he transforms into a polar bear. As soon as the bear is out of the katak he is (impossibly) on the sea-ice. Tulunigraq sings through the katak to the woman who won't marry; he then rises to seduce and marry her before chasing the sea-beast. All these events have shamanic or erotic import.

Underpinning the notion of katak-birth is the verb *ani*, which means both "to leave the iglu" and "to be born". This double meaning is beautifully expressed in a story current in Tikigaq but told here by inland people:

> The souls of two shamans are looking for a "clean and shining" woman through whom to be born. At last the elder one found a woman who was all shiny and all that could be seen were her spinal vertebrae. The inside of the woman was like a little house. There was a little katak, but it was so small that he never thought of going

out. Then one day he heard a voice, saying: "Come out! Come out!" And suddenly he got into a great hurry: he tumbled over to the katak and forced his way through the narrow passage.[4]

In the Raven and whale story a whale's soul was depicted as a woman in a whale which was an iglu; women's whaling ritual showed women animating their iglu whales; while the fragments of stories just listed show the birth-giving powers of the iglu katak, the woman here being depicted as an iglu in the process of delivery.

Returning to the whale hunt as a re-creation of the primal story, Tikigaq theory goes still further, to the realm of the primal "animal". Just as Tikigaq hunters dramatised the myth of Raven and the uiluaqtaq, so in the whale hunt the sea-beast came to life. As the following stories tell, this rebirth of the "animal" happened inside iglus.

THE WHALE-FLOAT IN THE IGLU

Before Kakianaq went out on the ice he took his crew into the skinboat and paddled it while they were still on land . . . Then they took the boat out to the water and Kakianaq's wife Suluk lay down on the ice while the crew paddled away and returned to where she was lying. Then they pretended to harpoon her.

As Suluk lay there she heard a whale rise. But she didn't look round. Kakianaq struck the whale immediately. Suluk heard what happened but she didn't look back. She got up and walked home over the sea-ice.

When Suluk came ashore she started to sing. I forget what song it was. I used to know it . . . As she walked she sang. And while she was singing a flock of ducks flew overhead. Suluk raised her arms and one of the ducks fell dead. She didn't use a sling or any other weapon: she just put up her hands. People said she must have power.

Suluk went home to her iglu and sat quietly. She knelt by the sleeping bench and rested her arms there. She put her head on her hands. Then she moved her head sideways. She was listening to something. What she heard was movement in the katak. It sounded like a float going round in circles in the katak. Suluk got up and looked. There was a whale-float in the katak. And, from the owner's mark, she saw it was her husband's.

Thinking no one would believe her when she told the story, Suluk took her drum and drum-stick and tied them to the float.

She tied them securely. This way everyone who saw it would know
it was hers and that the float had surfaced in her iglu . . .

This fragment of nineteenth-century history focuses on umialik
shamanism: the power lying within women's ritual inactivity. The two
earlier Raven stories depicted women who, in contrast to Raven's restless
movement, were passive and secluded. Here, in the eider duck episode,
the umialik's energy escapes the boundaries of ritual behaviour. Suluk
has lured a whale to her husband's ice-camp; now her exuberant *qilya*
(power) is impossible to contain. But once she has extended herself in
her electrifying upward gesture Suluk reverts to conventional inertia.

Just as Suluk lay with her head towards the village, so she returns
inland to persuade the whale to follow her. Out on the ice the woman
has enacted the whale as a victim; now she acts as whale soul in the
iglu whale.

Quiet as the woman remains, she and her husband are in balanced
partnership. As in Tulunigraq, women are in iglus, men meet in qalgis.
Each Tikigaq autumn this pattern is repeated; the same separation
recurs at whaling, where the ice-camp, worked by qalgi partners, was
called "qalgi". Women on land and men at sea thus constructed a field
through which the whales arrived in Tikigaq: first they came to the
men at their maritime meeting place; finally they entered the realm of
women. To summarise this final stage, the umialik couple's whale was
often called "hers".

The magic event in Suluk's iglu illustrates this balance of authority.
But the whale brought home through the shared operation implies a
third partner with a myth role. This third partner is the land itself.
Land, like the woman, is externally quiet but dynamic within. And like
all the symbols of the whale hunt land remains ambiguous. Woman is
the whale and whale soul, but woman remains woman. Her husband
is Tulunigraq, but he stays her husband. Tikigaq is primal sea-beast, its
iglus microcosmic versions of the whale and the sea-beast. When a
Tikigaq harpooner strikes the land whale stirs; when the katak gives
birth with the death of a bowhead the whale in the katak is both Tikigaq
nuna, and bowhead, and just katak.

The third story brings the symbol of the earth whale a step closer. Two
magical events take place here. First, a new symbol comes in: a dog that
transforms into a human. Later we shall see how the souls of the *wolf*
and whale were related. The dog was likewise propitious to whaling, and
most umialiks kept both dog- and wolf-skull amulets in their skinboats.
In the second magical event the dog harpoons the katak. Here the

birth-and-death entrance-and-exit hole comes into play. As though earth and whale were harpooned simultaneously, the iglu at once creates and kills the whale with which earth is mythically identified.

A WHALE HARPOONED IN THE IGLU KATAK

A man and wife had a son, and the son kept a puppy in their iglu. One day the father made a toy skinboat, complete with crew, for his son to play with. One night the couple noticed the young dog playing with the skinboat. It had taken the boat to the katak and was acting as umialik.

So they took off the dog's "parka" [fur] and hid it while the dog wasn't looking. But this was only after the crew in the toy skinboat had struck a whale through the katak. When the dog lost his parka the couple found they had a new son, though he'd once been a puppy.

The next morning, when these people woke, they heard shouting outside their iglu. "There's a dead whale floating in!" the people shouted. "It's coming straight towards your iglu!"

When they went outside they saw the whale approaching. It was floating by itself. There was no one towing. The man and woman told the people how their puppy played umialik at the katak. When they got to the whale they looked for the weapon. When they found it they knew this was the whale their dog harpooned in the katak. Their dog had harpooned a whale in their iglu.

A SHAMANESS RAISES A WHALE THROUGH THE KATAK

A man and woman lived in Tikigaq. They had no children.
One day the man came home from his qalgi,
and when he got home, he asked his wife to tell a story:
to tell an uqaluktuaq or an unipkaaq.
As soon as he got home he asked for the story.
But his wife said, "*You* tell a story! You were in the qalgi!
Men always tell stories in the qalgi!"
No, he wouldn't. And so he forced her to.
When she finally gave in, she said,
"I will tell a story. But you must keep it secret.
I will tell an unipkaaq."
The man said,

"It's the women who gossip when they come together . . . "
The man was getting angry. Then his wife said,
"You say you won't repeat it, so I'll tell an unipkaaq."
The man agreed he wouldn't repeat it . . .
Then the woman took off her parka and went to the katak.
She said, "Listen! And I'll tell you my unipkaaq."
The woman put her arm in the katak and stirred in a circle.
"Don't be scared when things start to happen," she said,
"You asked for an unipkaaq!"
Now as the woman stirred, they heard splashing.
It came from the katak,
and the entrance passage started filling with water.
The man saw water rising in the iglu.
Then the katak flooded.
"Don't be frightened" said the woman.
"Don't be frightened," she said as the man watched her.
Then something burst, and a whale appeared.
A whale rose in the katak, blocking the entrance.
It spouted in the katak.
"Since you'll keep this a secret, we can eat some," said the woman.
They ate part of it. They cut the whale up in the iglu . . .

The rest of the story is as follows. Next day the man goes to his qalgi and betrays his wife's secret. In revenge the woman raises water through the katak, floods the qalgi and drowns the men inside. Hearing of her prowess shamans fly in from the south to compete with her, but when they penetrate her iglu she destroys them. An avenging war party travels north, but this is repelled and the woman "cuts open the Point to bury the dead". Eventually the woman's brothers arrive to punish her. It turns out that she had been exiled to Tikigaq on account of previous murders in the south.

Suspended between an historically recognisable Tikigaq and myth-time, we are back in the archaic realm of the uiluaqtaq. This, however, is a married but unreformed uiluaqtaq, with a husband too weak to neutralise her magic. This woman, like the dual uiluaqtaq/grandmother of Tulunigraq's story, has both evil and creative aspects. As in the primal uiluaqtaq's iglu this power is kept isolated and secret. It is the husband, with his precariously authoritarian posture ("Now . . . tell me a story!") who tempts the woman to display her powers. And though the whale-conjuring is creative her contempt for her husband and the men in his qalgi is unambiguous.

Neither is there ambiguity in the woman, iglu and whale connection. No man is involved in this inland hunt, except as spectator. As though to pre-empt the mention of a "male" harpoon, all we are shown in the katak is a hand. The presence of the husband merely completes the male/female partnership through which whales must be captured. Otherwise it is the woman's whale, and the iglu, whale and woman we saw clustered in the Raven story, are re-created. Only the executive male is absent.

The symbol of the stirring hand is important. Every uiluaqtaq story presents a murderous shaman in the act of combing her hair or sewing. All the uiluaqtaq's suitors, bar her final husband, are killed with a version of this self-absorbed gesture. Given the predominance among Inuit of right-handedness, both sewing and combing are performed in sunwise (clockwise) circles. In the Sun and Moon story we saw how the spirits walked round the katak in sunwise motion before ascending to their places. The creative power of sunwise movement (as opposed to "widdershins", or anti-clockwise circles) was enacted in Tikigaq healing rituals and is folklorically widespread. Here the katak circling is both creative and dangerous; it raises a whale through Tikigaq nuna and destroys a qalgi. The circling hand in the watery katak repeats Raven Man's whale-float song ("Around, around, around!") which brought the diving land whale to the surface. It was the whale-float, too, as a symbol of the whale itself, that rose through Suluk's katak in the earlier story.

Finally there is the word "story" (*unipkaaq*: myth or legend). This the woman takes over from her husband's non-symbolic usage, loads it with mythological time and creational import, and moves straight to the centre of sacred time: to the heart of *the* story: the land whale's creation.

THE DRUM IN THE KATAK

A man is out whaling on the sea-ice, and his wife stays at home on the sleeping bench. Living with them in the iglu is the man's father. Using a shaman song to help him, the father seduces (or rapes) his son's wife, while the hunt is on.

When the husband returns, his drum, which is hanging on the iglu wall, starts to speak and repeats the father's song: "My daughter-in-law, let me lie with you: come!" The old man leaps up, seizes the drum and throws it through the katak into the passage. The son asks his wife to retrieve the drum, but when she looks for it the drum has vanished. That night the husband hangs himself.

Some time later a whale's carcass drifts in to Tikigaq, and a drum is found deep in its gullet. The wife recognises the drum her husband's father threw into the entrance passage. It had been the drum that killed the whale.[5]

Woman and iglu once again come together in the capture of a whale, and as before, though the story takes place at the time of the whale hunt, there is no male-executed harpooning. The first scene takes place during the female umialik's ritual sitting. The woman's sitting is violated in three ways: by infidelity, incest, and disruption of ritual chastity. This last transgression refers back to the original uiluaqtaq, whose own seclusion and virginity were destroyed by Raven Man. Important, too, is the equivalence between the hand-stirring of our last story and the drum in the katak. The round shamanic drum (*qilyaun*: "a device for power") was, as in most circum-polar cultures, associated with the sun, which via the katak-circling in the last story connects the uiluaqtaq with the circling sun spirit. It is as though the land whale story had assimilated its "sibling" creation myth, the Sun and Moon story.

But all this is secondary to the convergence of the iglu and the whale. The symbols follow one another with linear precision. The drum falls through the katak, and vanishes until it is retrieved in the mouth of the bowhead. Swallowed by the iglu through its passage and katak, the drum falls into both passage and whale. Iglu and whale have absorbed one another.

Part Two
The Ritual Year

SUMMER

Summer Stories

Samaruna said:
These small birds,
snow birds,
black and white ones,
ava-tali-guuvaq,
come to us from up there,
from the spirits.

While men hunt at sea,
and the women sit
quietly in the village,
the snow birds build
in the grass round our iglus.

Asatchaq:
While the men are on the sea-ice,
the avataliguuvaqs come.
Listen to the air!
The snow birds cheep!
Look into their iglus.
They leave down,
they leave shells.

Samaruna:
Little boys going hunting
in the spring and summer.
They hunt squirrels and longspurs
with their bows and lances.
But children never chase the snow bird.

It comes from the air.
It is small. We protect it.
Children! Never harm the avataliguuvaq!

Asatchaq:
When we were children, we told this story.
A snow bird sat crying on a hummock:

Someone has murdered my little husband!
A man, a hunter has killed my husband!

A big owl heard her cry.
He approached the snow bird. He sang:

What a fool you are to mourn
that little wretch,
with his spears of grass.
I'll be your husband!

The snow bird heard him and replied:
Marry an owl?
With those coarse feathers,
thick calves, thick beak,
domed forehead, neckless!

The owl was angry,
and pecked at her chest.
The snow bird cried *Arrii!* in pain.
But the owl just laughed:

That's women for you!
Sharp-tongued enough,
but poke one in the chest,
and she'll soon start to whimper!
And so they flew off in their separate directions.[1]

Samaruna:
Alla suli: I shall tell another.
Was it winter or summer?
A lemming came out of its hole one morning.
It looked round and shivered,
shook itself and sang:

The sky is a belly.
It arches round my burrow.
The air is clear.
No clouds up there.
But it's icy! icy!
Ya-ya! ya-YAI!
I'm freezing! FREEZING![2]

Summer is the season of emergence and movement. The sun is high;
the sea-ice drifts off; whaling is over; the wind comes from the south,
and the animals move with it.

While the whales were running they filled the minds of Tikigaq hunters. As spring turns to summer the world comes alive with smaller species.

Eider duck, old squaw, harlequin and scoters pour north to breed in the marshes and wetlands. Guillemots home in on their nesting ledges. Gulls and kittiwakes crowd back with them.

Geese and cranes wing through in V-formation. Eagles and falcons nest on river bluffs and sea cliffs. Plovers and whimbrel, snipe and phalarope raise their young on the coast and the tundra. Owls hunt in the midnight sunshine.

As soon as the whale hunt and the whaling feast are over the whole village moves out to the south shore to hunt *ugruk* (bearded seal) and walrus.

Ugruk and walrus have just come north, and hunters stalk them as they bask on the ice-floes. Every umialik needs sealskin to cover his boat-frame for next year's whale hunt. The dark meat, dried and then soaked in seal oil, is eaten all summer.

So while the south wind blows and the sun is high, Tikigaq
    decamps:
  each family to its place where the ancestors hunted:
  tents – used boatskins patched with caribou –
    standing high on the beach-head in the long spring grasses.

Here, among the vertebrae and hip-bones from old seal hunts,
    and the poppies, saxifrage, anemones and willowherb
  that have pushed through the tundra between stones and
    driftwood,
  the women sew their families' gut-skin parkas
  and the waterproof boots they'll need all summer.
  And the old have come out, after winter in their iglus:
  the men weaving fish nets, women braiding strands of sinew,
  while children, barefoot, chase squirrels and longspurs:

      "Sigirik! Sigiriiraq!
        Come out little parka squirrel!"
      "Qupaluk! Qupaluk!
        Qain Qupaluuraq!
      And you, little longspur!"

Flubbering their lips, they whistle and banter with the species
    that came out or migrated with the final bowhead,
  running through the night sun, only sleeping in the skin tent
    when the women's south-shore stories reach them.

"This is the path," the grandmother finishes,
    brushing a hand along the south beach [*nali*],
"poor boys, back then, took on journeys to seek visions.
    No one knows where those orphans came from:
whether they were really people, and what animals helped them.
    They started at nali: in dogskins, no boots, hungry:
walking alone, and sleeping with the owls and ptarmigan.
    At Imnat, they met spirits who forced them to play games –
challenged them to dance and wrestle,
    run up the cliffs with whales on their backs –
who made traps with bones and axes and whose songs made
            them dizzy.
    They met brown bears and wolves that hunted them in circles.
They were eaten and coughed back; they became great shamans.
    They walked on. They found uiluaqtaqs on the tundra,
who hunted with their combs, and had teeth in their *utchuks*.
    Any poor boy who had *qilya* [shaman power] beat the spirits at
            their own games,
turned the traps on their owners and stole them as amulets,
    harpooned and married the women who attacked them,
and walked home at snow-fall, to sleep till whaling . . . "
Below, where the beach meets the sea-ice,
    dog-sleds travel, carrying meat to umialiks' caches.
Hunters steer between the ice-floes,
    moor their kayaks, track, crawl, spring out and harpoon
the sleeping ugruk, call for their partners,
    tow carcasses behind their kayaks, while the hunter who
            has struck,
cries out to his wife in the voice of the animal
    whose spirit helps him and whose amulet he carries.
The women cry back from their tents across the sea-ice,
    walk down, sharpening their knives, help drag the seal in,
butcher it, and peg the scraped skin on the tundra.

TIKIGAQ TRAVELLERS

When the ice has drifted and there's open water,
    it is time to travel.
The old people stay on shore or pitch their tents in Tikigaq,
    where they'll fish, and raid duck nests,
net sea-trout from the beaches, and walk inland to pick berries.

Now the skinboats are loaded with nets, harpoons and ugruk rope,
    bags of seal oil, baleen, ivory and whale meat;
the men run the prow across the beach shelf, leap in to their benches,
    cram the children between women, puppies, harness, tent skins,
and finally the steersman, the umialik, thrusts off with his paddle,
    and the dogs on shore are scolded into hauling by the woman
        who runs with them,
as the crew heads down-coast across surf and current.

Before Imnat, they come in, visit kinsfolk's places, qalgi partners,
    eat, sit with legs stretched, dry their parkas,
watch the guillemots' low feeding lines fly out for the horizon,
    study the grey whale, offshore, and the orca ["sea wolf"]
        hunting,
back-fin, like the moon, scrawled grey, that signifies inua.
    The women shout, as the orca feed, in clouds of seal blood,
"Leave some for me!" they call to its inua,
    and run through the water, laughing, to grab lumps of blubber.

At Pinuatchiaq, they stop to scan the marshes from the high ground,
    and the sky at Imnat – if the cliffs are swollen there will be good
        weather –
then straight on to Isuk, where the flat land meets the first cliffs,
    and the beach is cut by running water.
They camp here, drink, eat whaleskin and ugruk, listen to the
        guillemot
– a bird with no soul because there are too many –
    and whoop back "*Arru! Arru!*" to them:
massed cries pierced by kittiwakes and ravens.

Next they take the boats round, and land at Sisu where the cliffs
        are ruined.
    The men climb the scree until they reach the nesting ledges,
scale knots and fissures, hang from their fingers,
    clouds of birds rise, showering them with faeces,
the men stuffing eggs in their parka bellies,
    for the women to boil over beach-fires at Isuk,
while those who felt giddy when they first tried climbing,
    walk up the west side, and let rope out for their partners,
who dangle from the cliff-top to scoop birds with pole-nets.

Samaruna said:
Two men, they say, in an ancestor story,
who shared their wives,

were hunting at Imnat
as they always did in partnership.
And the one on the cliff-top let his partner down,
and then untied the rope that held him.
"Stay down and die!" he shouted,
"I'm taking your woman!"
The man on the cliff hung on all summer,
eating guillemots' and gulls' eggs.
When skinboats passed,
his shouts were drowned by wind and sea-birds.
But round his neck, the man wore an amulet,
a brown-bear-snout amulet,
and one night, he took the bear's snout
and chewed it, to liven it with his saliva.
Soon enough he heard a voice above him.
Somebody was calling him.
"Here's rope for you! Climb!
Your wife and partner have gone home already.
Grab this and climb!"
The man tied the rope round his waist.
He reached the cliff-top.
There was a brown bear, his amulet animal.
The bear had lowered its intestines and pulled the man up
    with them.
The bear said:
"Here I am: your *tupitkaq, your aanguaq*, your *anatkuq*.*
That's why I've saved you."
The bear left for the hills,
and the man walked back to Tikigaq.
He found his wife, and killed his partner.
He'd become a shaman.

The travellers go round the cliffs and past the land controlled by Tikigaq. They hunt all the way, and cache what they'll need in late summer or autumn. Slowly they move on to the trade fair at Sisualik, a sand spit a hundred and thirty miles south of Tikigaq.

At Sisualik they meet southern Inupiaqs, inland river hunters, island people. Maritime travellers bring whale meat, seal meat, blubber, ugruk skins and ivory. Inlanders bring black-bear meat, dried salmon, caribou and furs from the mammals of the river valleys: fawn skins, marten,

---

* Your magical familiar, amulet animal, shamanistic helping spirit.

muskrat, red and cross fox, wolf, wolverine and lynx. For three weeks of July and August hundreds of families camp in small village compounds, hunting belukha, exchanging goods with inherited partners, and forging new contacts.

The high ground on the spit is thick with berries, and beyond the lines of skinboats, tents and kayaks, the villagers hold races and games of endurance; there are contests between shamans, spouse exchanges, dances, storytellings, while strangers from the far side* arrive quietly, barter reindeer pelts, glass beads, copper and tobacco for Inupiaq goods and then leave quickly.

> The poor, who have no skinboats, travel east on foot,
>   in bands, where the caribou take them,
> children in their mothers' parkas, dogs with the tent skins, poles
>   and side packs.
>   Behind the cliffs, they climb the hill-tops –
> flints and fossil-coral grinding their boot-soles –
>   walking north-east for the valleys where the game feeds,
> setting traps for wolf, fox, marmot, lynx and wolverine.

> Over the hill, they hear loons on the river,
>   watch peregrines hunt from the bluffs of Kuukpak,
> below, through mosquitoes, the tundra stretches, brown and purple,
>   ravens quarrelling with foxes over caribou the wolves have taken,
> the half-sunk antlers' rib-spread arched in hunger,
>   wind rushing through them.
> The men stalk, singing *taqsiun* [lure songs]: "Qa-in! Approach!
>   Qa-in! Qa-in!"
>   herd the caribou through lakes and rivers
> where they chase them in kayaks; line migration tracks
>   with cairns and drive them into gulleys.
> Eating and drying out the meat all night at sunlit hill camps,
>   they skirt the routes their enemies have taken,
> and the graves of murdered children whose teeth they hear grinding.

> Then there is the outcast, poor boy,
>   who was thrown away, and lived with the dogs in ruined iglus,
> and who travels alone, to return as a shaman.
>   The outcast walks hungry. The wind cuts his parka;
> his boots rot in the marshes. The dream from his mind extends
>   to where the sky meets tundra, waking vision, never sleeping

---

* Siberian Chukchis, who by the seventeenth century had European wares.

while the daylight fills his body,
   sky pours through the sutures and the eye-holes, thorax hollows,
and he sees his skeleton, ablaze and freezing, numbering the
        bones, knows them,
   calling each by name until it sings its answer,
identifies the life-souls clustered at the joints and organs,
   tastes self-meat, comprehending it has died, continues living:
same, no different from companion species,
   and he lies down with the ptarmigan and foxes:
intercourse and inanition: thighs smeared with feathers,
   fox eats his tongue, eyes, heart and liver,
bird-wife escapes with his usuk and testes:
   dog-mother history vomited on stream-bed,
dry with vertebrae, and amulets the moon excreted.

The animals take pity, and undo his ligaments,
   the guts are dried and knotted around tundra hummocks,
jerked towards the light by raven, into winter by the peregrine,
   scavenging his colon, they peck and trample,
leaving the skin empty and his mind in a circle.

Another, destitute, leaves Tikigaq: abandons his weapons,
   joins the wolves, and learns to speak their language,
runs all summer with them, along rivers, with the lame and pregnant,
   eating rodents and foxes, takes a wife among them, a young
        woman,
who fucks and then eats him.
   Then the wolf umialik calls him and approaches,
butts his wolf skull on the tundra,
   scrapes back the wolf-mask, showing his inua,
the round face-disc, nameless person-spirit, naked, radiant, saying:

"You humans, who have seen us become human, animals
   and human, who have lived with us and shared our food,
who have wives among our people and who know our children:
   you who have come, you'll return to your own people,
and with what you have seen, invite the wolf soul
   to your rituals and dances, so those first times – separated from us
when humans were animals and animals were people –
   are made whole in your story, when you tell them what your
        dream was.

"Go back now. You are one of us. Because of your visit,
   you have made us happy. You have joined us. Thank you.

When you were a child, and had no kin, your hunger drove you
      from the village.
Now you are a shaman. You will tell your people how to treat us.
Whenever you sing, you'll remember your wife and your kinsmen
      among us.
And when you hunt the whale in spring, we will help you.
"All this, because you have visited our people.
    But don't be like those other shamans who come once and then
      leave us
and say nothing, leave the story broken, and forget to revisit us."
The soft, thick hood slips back and the wolf umialik vanishes.
    Home in Tikigaq, the young shaman sleeps all winter:
mind curled in the earth-wound,
    dreams of whale's flukes breaching in the iglu.
They'll catch whales next season.

These journeys took place in the single two-month day of summer,
whose warmer weather and unbounded space, with no sunsets or
divisions, offered temporary freedom, both of movement and from
social pressure.

    Isolated in extended families on the tundra and the beaches, people
escaped the tensions of the village: the malice of neighbours, jealous
rivals, shame and failure, inherited feuds, and, not least, angry shamans
inadvertently offended whose retribution they continually expected.

So in summer they went out. They were out:
    dropped ritual trappings and taboo imperatives.
Absolved from the absolute and lunar inspection,
    they left at home those forms which,
like the string games[3] patterning their stories,
    implicated a commitment to high communal projects.
So now, the whale hunt over and the moon in abeyance,
    summer was pragmatic, secular, the dream agnostic.

AUTUMN

Much of the summer is damp and stormy. By August it starts to grow dark again. As the days get shorter the tundra hardens. Ground-hugging plants turn scarlet and crimson; bearberries, cloudberries and blueberries ripen.

There are flurries of snow. The migrants take off; brown bear retreat to their dens above Imnat; solitary gulls and ravens scavenge.

Travellers stop at river mouths to take salmon. They hunt caribou for short-haired autumn skins; retrieve any meat they had stored in the summer; pick berries and raid lemmings' nests for tubers.

High seas make skinboat travel dangerous. By the time the people are home in September the nights are dark, the sun stays low, and the moon has re-established its presence.

Back on the Point the men hunt the last migrating duck and geese; old people and women snare ptarmigan and squirrels; when the sea has been high the children gather tomcod and sea-slugs stranded on the beaches. Otherwise, fresh food is limited.

A quiet period follows. Equipment taken out in the summer has been used up, broken or abandoned. Frozen meat, skins and trade goods fill Tikigaq's caches. The village reassembles. Kinsfolk regroup in their iglu clusters. The men get ready to open their qalgis.

DAYLIGHT AND DARKNESS

Asatchaq said:
When he made land,
and the world was still dark,
Raven heard the people talking about daylight.
Everything was dark.
No sun. No moon.

But inland was a man who kept daylight in his iglu.
This man lived alone.
He lived with a daughter.
They hoarded the daylight in their iglu.
Tulunigraq travelled. He went to find it.
He went inland, till he found the iglu.

He entered.
He went into the passage.
When he looked up through the katak,
he saw two bags hanging. Skin-bags.
One held the darkness.
The other held daylight.

The man's daughter sat there.
Tulunigraq used thought.
He used his thought to make the daughter play.
The daughter nagged her father.
"Let me play with that ball!" the daughter nagged him.
This went on. Until the man gave in.
He took down the bag that held the daylight.
The daughter played with it.
The ball was made of caribou.
The girl pushed the ball towards the katak.
Her father tried to stop her.
"*Naagga!* No!"
The girl pushed the ball further . . .
it went down through the katak.

Tulunigraq was there.
He caught it.
He ran through the passage;
ran with daylight.

Tulunigraq was Raven.
He had a raven's bill.
He tore the skin-ball.
Tore at daylight.
Running through the willows.
Raven looked behind him.

The daylight man chasing him.
The man was a falcon.
He was Peregrine falcon.
Peregrine ran. He shouted:
"PITQIKTUAQ! TRICKSTER!
You'll be dead when I get you!
THIEF! PITQIKTUAQ! YOU TRICKSTER!"
"QAAA!" shouted Raven.
"You'll be dead when I get you!"

Raven got into some willow bushes.
Raven tore the skin-ball.
Peregrine was on him.
But the ball flew open.
QAUGAA SILA! DAWN ROSE ON HIM!
DAYLIGHT!

"UUNUKPUAQ! UUNUKPUAGMUN: DARKNESS!"
cried the one-who-said-darkness.

"QUAGAA: LIGHT ON EVERYTHING!"
said Raven.
"NIGHT!" cried Peregrine.
"DAYLIGHT!" said Raven.

"DARKNESS!"
            "DAYLIGHT!"
"DARKNESS!"
            "DAYLIGHT!"

And so they went on shouting
"Daylight!" "Darkness!"
Raven *made* daylight.
There was light in the sky.
So we have both now.
(Raven went on shouting,
"Daylight for the earth!
Daylight for nuna!")

It would be no good,
if we had the one and not the other.

Samaruna added:
The animals fought. They threw light and darkness.
Daylight and darkness came into balance.

Asatchaq said:
Winter follows summer. Two halves.
Light and darkness complete one another.
This story follows.

HOW RAVEN BECAME BLACK

Long ago, when animals were people,
Raven and Loon were partners.
They agreed to tattoo each other.

"Me first," said Raven.
(He was white at the beginning.)
So Raven took lamp soot
and drew little fire sparks
on his partner's feathers.
That was how Loon
got the pattern on his feathers.

But Raven tired of painting.
He grabbed some soot and ashes
and tossed them over Loon's back.
That's why it's grey now.

Loon was angry.
He scooped soot from a pot
and threw it at Raven.

Raven had been white.
Now he's black.
He stayed that way.
There's no more to this story.[4]

RUMINATION ON

THE TWO-PART SHAPE OF THINGS, THE COUNTERPOINT OF OPPOSITES, PATTERNS, PARTI-COLOURS, STREAKS AND TATTOOING

Tikigaq notebook, 12 January 1976

I ask Asatchaq: "What happened to the second skin-ball Raven saw hanging in the light man's iglu?"

Asatchaq grunts and passes a hand over his stubble. The gesture is ambiguous, absent, perhaps evasive or hostile. The old man encourages my questions. His responses are either precise and immediate or a ramble into subtexts, reminiscences, genealogies and shaman-lore. But sometimes, as here, he avoids my question, and I am left with the story. It hangs between us, opaque like the skin-ball. I want to tear the story open: flood the old man's half-lit cabin with archaic meaning. Asatchaq just looks at me and mutters, "That's a true story. You must learn it."

So I must accept the story's presence, without explanation. I must both believe and believe *in* the stories, inherit what he, at my age, fifty years ago, learned from Samaruna. Thus he leads me slowly round my querying, querulous Western persona. I am the grandson. The two of us are ataatagiik: "grandpa-and-another". Like meat, I must consume the stories. And when I've consumed them, the stories will eat me. Their presence will become real, a part of my brain's domestic topography. So he forces my retreat. I must enter the iglu of what he tells me.

There hangs the skin-ball. Darkness encloses. But light, too, streams from the bushes where Raven scrabbles. Daylight and darkness fuck and struggle. They're jointed, separate and articulated. Fighting. Married.

Under his bare lamp Asatchaq dozes. "You see," the breath sings, "they are one and two things, daylight and darkness, simultaneously."

Man and woman: daylight and darkness

Summer and winter, light and darkness, are in high relief with one another. When Raven challenged the primordial night-time he brought daylight to counterpoint, not destroy, the darkness. Like darkness, daylight was a primal substance. The two co-existed. But like the uiluaqtaq's sexuality, daylight was hoarded, sterile and useless.

Tulunigraq stole light so humanity could prosper. But the aim of the theft was also the elemental order. For all things to cohere there must be partnership. The parts of the whole must be in counterpoint, balance and mutual contention. Without this stress of two – the divisible unity whose parts lived at once in divorce and conjugation – the cosmos would be sterile. As Asatchaq said at the end of Raven's story, "It would be no good if we had light without the darkness."

Often this dialectic is unpleasant. Even the hemispheres of earth and sky grind harshly together. But from the percussion of unlike halves new life emerges. Raven clashes with the uiluaqtaq. From their union the land whale rises. Raven violates the daylight ball and daylight escapes to balance the darkness.

Brother and sister in the Sun and Moon story likewise merge. Siblings in coitus, theirs is a partnership of both total unity and violation. The absolute conjunction of sexuality and kinship is translated to eternal separation. The criminal trickster becomes the lunar deity. His generative but fickle power flows from oneness experienced, and then ruined.

This universal pattern is repeated in small, earthly replicas. The plumage of peregrine falcon, owl, loon and bunting, their streaks, flecks and speckles, are daylight and darkness mixed and in counterpoint. Raven was white before Loon threw soot at him: Raven's transformation – like daylight become darkness – reverses his own exploit. To remedy his lost condition he cries out for the daylight. (Loon's feathers are called "fire sparks". The crone made Raven with burned oil and feathers.)

"LIGHT!" shouted Raven.
    "DARKNESS!" cried Peregrine.
Designing daylight and darkness,
    they hurl "Darkness!" "Daylight!"
Their words are soot.
    They tattoo the cosmos.

Soot is also inscribed on the Sun and Moon story. The sun and moon tattoo each other. The sun sister smears her brother with lamp soot, then mutilates herself with her *ulu* – a half-moon-shaped slate knife used by women. When, in post-myth-time, the sun first rises after the winter solstice, the sister is still streaked with blood; the moon's face is patched in its black and white phases.

When round-faced Tikigaq girls first menstruate the skin between the mouth and chin is mutilated. An old woman, an aana, draws thread soaked with lamp-soot in three vertical black lines down the girl's chin, and tattoos it.

Tattoos and sexual bleeding
    tie her to the sister.
Tattooing is soot smears, fire-sparks,
    speckles, the sun's streaking.
And daubed like her brother,
as she raises her face to *tatqim inua*,*
    the woman is his separated, sublunary replica.

Land and sea: birth-things and grave goods

Tikigaq children were given social and symbolic identity in their first weeks of life. This earliest period was spent with the mother in a tiny birth hut. Here the mother and child lived together until the mother's period of taboo was over. But the child's isolation was broken by an important visitor who would be the baby's spiritual guardian (*qumnaaluk*). The guardian brought gifts that were both physical and symbolic. First there was a set of protective animal amulets.

Then the guardian brought names – he or she liked to be the baby's namesake – and a set of food taboos. Most boys, for example, were

* The moon spirit, Alinnaq.

forbidden whale meat in some form or in some circumstance until they were adults. Equally important was the child's birth or death amulet group (discussed below). Finally the guardian inducted the baby into life membership of his or her football team.

Tikigaq's ball-game was a mixture of rugby, soccer and all-in wrestling. It was played in midwinter on full-moon nights. The field stretched from the tip of the Point along the south shore towards the mainland.

Everyone in Tikigaq belonged to one of two teams. There was the team that ran *inland* from the Point, and the team that ran *seaward* from inland.

The more intricate rules of Tikigaq football are forgotten. But besides kicking and running with the ball in your team's direction, the nature of the game was symbolic.

Picking up a skin-ball and escaping with it in the darkness recalls Raven's theft of light. In fact all the central football images correspond to that primal light-theft moment: skin-ball, escape; even the two hanging balls, one shining and one dull, converge on the contrast of skin-football and full moon.

Meshed with these images is a second, more schematic group of symbols. This is the inland and seaward opposition: a widespread and taboo-fraught tension among Inuit, which Tikigaq's long seaward finger made especially poignant.

Many Inuit saw land and sea as charged with mutually contagious spiritual force. This meant that land and sea products must be kept separate, or the game would be offended. Fear of retribution from animal spirits was expressed in taboos, and most Inuit societies had variants of roughly the same character. Some of the most common forbade women to sew caribou skins on the sea-ice; others ruled out eating freshwater fish with whale or seal meat.

Tikigaq had several rituals which expressed land–sea contrast, while also denying any related taboo imperatives. One of the highest moments of the whale hunt itself expresses this precisely. When the whale has been killed the woman umialik walks down to the sea-ice carrying a slice of cooked maktak (whale skin and blubber) on a piece of raw caribou stomach. Her crew proceeds to eat the two together before butchering the whale. The following rite, involving the death of a wolfcub, also evoked both whale and the land whale story.

The wolfcub sacrifice and wolf and whale

There was a pond near the sea end of the village with an island in the middle: a small patch of earth that rose through the water. Here, each autumn, while the qalgi rituals ran, a wolfcub brought from inland was tied to a stake with a sealskin thong. When the first seal of the winter had been taken the wolf was slaughtered. Nothing further is remembered.

The pattern of the wolfcub sacrifice harmonises so completely with its symbolism that perhaps the pond and its island were artificial. No one knows; and the site has disappeared.

In structure, the wolf island replicates both the separation and adjacency of sea and land. Just as Tikigaq is surrounded – at least on three sides – by the sea, so the island was both touched by the water and separate from it. This paradox pointed to the rhythm of Tikigaq people's own affiliation. In the summer they were, for the most part, inland hunters. Return to the village marked return to their coastal identity. The moment of sacrifice suggested this seasonal and geographic change. The wolf's death confirmed their removal from land territory and the onset of sea-ice hunting.

But since pond and island also suggested contiguity of sea and nuna, clash co-existed with reconciliation.

Just as shamans controlled spirits too dangerous for the laity to handle, so Tikigaq's manipulation of these symbolic ideas, and ritual synthesis of otherwise dangerous polarisations, had a certain shamanistic bravura.

Tikigaq dealt precisely thus with land/sea taboos. Far from keeping land and sea things separate, Tikigaq – acknowledging the power inherent in the grand antitheses – rejoiced in convergence. Apart from one insignificant rule against dropping loose caribou hair into cracks in the sea-ice, people lived confidently within the very tension that engendered anxiety in other groups.

Tikigaq also broke land/sea taboos kept by Inuit elsewhere. Far from being outlawed, caribou meat and caribou-skin parkas were actively demanded on the ice at whaling. In bold taboo reversal, people skewered bits of whale meat and fish together for their children during the most sacred period of autumn rituals. To accompany this gesture – a recipe for disaster among many other Inuit – they contrived an ambiguous and mildly sadistic joke. Before feeding the children, they tricked them by confusing a term for frozen fish with the name – a near homonym for the fish word – of the sacred objects which were next on the ritual programme (*quluguluguq*).

The wolfcub ritual pointed to another dual character. Just as land and sea were both separate and one, so land and whale were two before they were unified. The land became and remained a whale. But why sacrifice a wolf to mark the end of the inland period, and not a fox, a caribou fawn or a marmot? Each of these is an inland creature.

The wolf and the whale in Inuit legend were mystically twinned. Every umialik kept wolf-skull amulets in his skinboat during whaling. The leader of the Itivyaaq whale-hunting spirits was a wolf-tailed being. As we shall see in the story that follows, the wolf soul was in fact the whale soul's double. So just as the little island was more than an island, so the wolfcub itself was wolf in form only. When a hunter ritually slaughtered the wolf, symbolically he killed a whale. The blood of the wolf on Tikigaq nuna presaged next spring's whale hunt, when real whales would be brought to the myth whale's body.

One connection between wolf and whale may be found in the orca ("killer whale"), known in Tikigaq as "sea wolf" because like the wolf the orca often hunts in packs. These packs, in turn, were associated with whale-hunting crews. Aviq told me: "Sometimes in the summer you see eight of those *aagluks* [orcas] like the eight men in a skinboat."

Unlike some Indian hunters of south-east Alaska, Tikigaq never hunted orca. People talked, on the contrary, of orca "hunting for the people". Watching orca feed offshore, people shouted, "Leave me some meat with a lump of fat on it!" Sometimes the orca would move on, leaving half-eaten seals to drift ashore.

Asatchaq said:
Aagluk is part human.
We know this from the aagluk's fin.
It rises through the water.
It has black and white markings.
Marks like the moon's face.
This face on aagluk's fin is its inua.
This is the face of its human spirit.
That's why we talk to it.

Samaruna:
The moon spirit comes from Tikigaq.
Whales come from the moon.
The wolf and the whale have one soul.
Tikigaq's a whale.

Asatchaq:
This story is about a wolfskin.

It's about two brothers who caught many whales.
They were both umialiks.
The brothers' names were Qiikigaq and Qiikiaaluk.
They lived here in Tikigaq with their father.

And their father had a dream.
A man came to fetch him.
He took him to the sea-ice.
The man who came to fetch him
had an iglu underneath the sea-ice.
So he went.
And when they were inside, the man said,
"Your son will catch a wolf this winter.
Just one. Not two.
But once you've skinned it, don't cut the skin or use it.
Do as I say, and you'll catch a whale.
Your son and his brother will catch a whale each, every spring."
The younger brother, Qiikiaaluk, caught a wolf that winter.
And next spring the two brothers caught a whale each.
But they never cut the wolfskin –
not even for the whale feast.
Next winter Qiikiaaluk caught another wolf, an even finer one.
And next spring the brothers caught two whales each.

Then Qiikiaaluk caught a third wolf.
This wolf was finer than the two he'd caught already.
And after he'd caught this,
the brothers each took three whales in the spring.
This happened every year.
Next season the brothers caught four whales each.
And after that, five . . . those two brothers . . .

And when the number of whales reached ten,
Qiikiaaluk caught another wolf, as he'd done each winter.
It was the finest of all.

And Qiikigaq, his older brother,
cut the skin for their wives
to wear as ruffs at the whale feast.
The two brothers had killed ten whales each.

But after the last wolfskin was cut Qiikiaaluk fell sick.
And that spring the brothers died.

They'd caught ten whales each.
But the spring they died they caught none at all.

And when the brothers died,
the man who'd fetched their father came to fetch him again.
He took him to his iglu in the water.
And when the old man went inside the iglu,
he saw the last wolfskin hanging on the iglu wall.
That's the length of it.

Birth and death amulets

The guardian's final gift to the newborn child was its amulet affiliation. Almost everyone in Tikigaq belonged to one of two groups: those whose amulets were powered by *birth*-things; and people with amulets livened by *death*-stuff or grave goods.

No one owned or carried a birth or death amulet. Birth and death were forces that lent power to other amulets: eagle-head, foxtail, loonskin, whale or walrus effigy. The animal soul within the amulet would be the owner's helping partner. But in sickness or danger the amulet owner could seek birth or death powers.

This was done by benign contagion. A birth-group member (*igniruaqtuqtuq*: "carries an amulet powered by childbirth") chewed his amulet and then rubbed it on an umbilical cord, a dried placenta, a pregnant woman, or a woman with a newborn baby.

Members of the death class (*qunuqtuqtuq*) rubbed their amulets on human corpses, bones, or the goods that lay with the dead on their burial racks. Amulets, thus charged and applied to the body, released healing protection.

Within this system lay a counter-current. Birth people were allergic, often fatally, to death-stuff; birth-things were dangerous to the members of the death class. Several stories tell how shamans reversed the lethal power of "meat that had touched a dangerous opposite", given them by enemies. To make social life possible for mixed amulet class families children were immunised with light early contact with an opposite substance.

The population thus lived within a pattern of contrary absolutes. But as though to spice its perfect, all-embracing symmetry there was a sub-group, an offshoot of the two other classes.

The people who belonged to this small third group carried sealskin menstrual pads (*agliqtuqtuq*). Owners of dried menstrual amulets (*makaun*) were partially connected to both amulet classes. They belonged with the birth class in that blood, like babies, came from the vagina. They were related to the non-birth death class because menstruation is non-generative. At once disrupting the birth–death symmetry, the pad was thus also a point of convergence.

Within the menstrual pad lay a further paradox. Just as Tikigaq modified the law of land/sea separation, so menstrual-pad owners – male hunters especially – transcended the most absolute of all taboos. For vaginal blood horrified the animals.

In Tikigaq this meant that menstruating women were barred from the sea-ice and forbidden to touch game. The bold reversal of this taboo – albeit in specialised cases of menstrual-pad ownership – was yet another instance of the daring with which Tikigaq manipulated its metaphysical sanctions.

Converging forces of the present, past and future lay behind the birth and death idea. On account of their power to bear children and, by menstruating, to scare off animals – there was the power of women. *Birth* also drew on souls of future beings. *Death*, on the other hand, evoked ancestral spirits that would manifest in future rebirths.

This circuit of helping spiritual forces also created a gigantic emblem proclaiming the nature of individual and collective existence. Birth and death were opposites, ran counter, clashed, and mutually denied each other. But they also embodied a single, continuous generative system, within which life-giving women, their babies and the forebears belonged, ever present, to the on-going present, with its ambiguities and dangers.

The shamanistic function of the birth/death system was not, however, confined to individual amulet members. Just as birth/death events – and among them "whale hunting in the iglu" – were mediated by the iglu passage and katak, so the birth/death system was deployed in the spring whale hunt.

> *Asatchaq said:*
> Before leaving the village,
> when the paddles were clean,
> my father took a dark stone, *aumaa*,
> and he marked each paddle.
>
> I've looked for that stone
> in the hills
> and on river-beds.
> I never found it.

Aumaa is graphite, lumps of which were gathered in the summer, kept from year to year in amulet bags and used by umialiks to mark their eight skinboat paddles.

Two bands of graphite were drawn across the freshly scraped and whittled blade:

> Birth was a short line
>   at the blade tip.
> Longer and above this,
>   death was drawn parallel.

The condition of the paddles was important because the paddles moved within the water and were exposed to the whale's view. While the crew and the boat-ribs were masked by sealskins, the blades nakedly proclaimed the hunters' condition. On the one hand, their fresh wood radiated ritual purity. Aggressively, however, their graphite marks declared that birth and death had been brought together and were hunting in tandem.

This threat was balanced by two reassurances. First that the hunt took place within, and was part of, a symmetrically ordered dialectic. Second, that birth and death had been reconciled; and that rebirth would follow the whale's death immediately.

The other hunting tackle that physically went closest to the whale was the drag-float system. This consisted of the three inflated sealskins (*avataqpak*) which would buoy the harpooned whale as the boat continued to pursue it.

So before the crew went out on the ice, and before the skins were finally inflated, life or death amulet contact was applied to the whale-floats. The umialik husband did this at home with a woman helper.

> *Asatchaq:*
> If he was a birth group man,
> the umialik called a woman who had just had a baby.
> If his amulet worked with death-things,
> the woman must come from an iglu
> where someone had died recently.

Like the events in supernatural whaling stories, the ritual involved woman, a whale-float and movement through the iglu. But here the point of transition was the skylight, not the passage or katak. The ritual was quite brief and simple.

Samaruna:
The woman stood on the iglu roof.
The umialik went inside the iglu.
When both of them were ready,
the woman took the sealskin rope,
and raised the whale-floats
through the skylight.

In this way the drag-floats were *born* from the iglu, and their owner's amulet identity was confirmed by a woman. Her opposite gender to the male umialik's made his birth or death association with the drag-floats fertile.

Graphite tattoos on clean male paddles
    answer her
three soot streaks.

Sister/Brother: husband/wife.
    They'll catch a whale
when the sun has risen.

Opening the Qalgis

There were six qalgis in the village and everyone belonged to one of them. When a boy, around puberty, could shoot a bow and arrow he started going to his father's. Women joined their husband's qalgi when they married.

A boy's hair was tonsured.
The corners of his lower lip were pierced,
and ivory labrets inserted.
When girls had menstruated,
three lines of soot were tattooed on their faces.

Once they were home in the autumn, men and women separated. Women went to the family iglu, men went to their qalgis, where they bailed out any water that had melted through the permafrost in the summer weather.

Once they had cleaned their iglus and qalgis they lit the stone oil lamps. This was the first act of the ritual season. It was done as follows.

A boy from each qalgi was chosen to fetch lamp wicks. Dressed in a seal-gut parka, he walked to his iglu and waited at his family's skylight.

When the women heard him rattling his parka, they handed up wicks of rolled moss they'd gathered on the tundra. The boy took these back for the qalgi oil lamps.

When the buildings were dry, and the women were busy sewing winter boots and parkas, the men started work in the qalgis on their weapons and equipment.

They'd brought home tree trunks from the south shore, willow branches from the Kuukpak valley, gathered flints and slate on the cliffs and hill-tops, dug mastodon and fossil ivory by rivers and beaches; hauled in rocks to press the edges of the skylight membrane, and dragged home whale-jaws, ribs and vertebrae to build into their entrance-passages.

Some worked on tools. They made adzes, chisels, burins, wedges, hammers, bow drills, arrow flakers. They carved ice picks, meat hooks, shovels, scoops and ladles made of antler, musk-ox horn and mastodon ivory.

Men worked on broad slate whale harpoon blades, long flint spear-heads, skin rope, fish nets, slings and fowling tackle.

They made harpoon floats and wound plugs, toggles, scrapers, dog-sled harness, short knives, straight and crescent bladed, long flensing tools of sharp polar-bear bone, three-piece compound bows lashed with sinew and baleen, arrows straightened hot through vertebrae and fletched with seabird feathers.

Some worked outside on baleen sleds for winter hunting, or long sleds for the skinboat, with ivory runners. Umialiks repaired their inherited old boat-frames; their men scraped clean and smoothed new paddles.

Excepting the boat, all last year's whaling tackle had been burned in the summer. Next spring's equipment must be fresh for the whaling season. Otherwise the whales would smell dirt and be disgusted.

The shamans worked. They sang. They made amulets and masks and divination tackle, steamed and hooped drum frames, fitted their handles with wolf-heads, whale flukes, spirit faces.

And while the men carved, flaked, lashed, drilled, wedged and hammered, and the old men slept or sat doing nothing, and equipment lay scattered in the wood and baleen shavings, among stone chips, jade from the Kobuk River, flakes of ivory, and the men ate food the women brought.

One man stood on the qalgi roof: he watched the sun's progress until, travelling low, the sun's rim touched the Point, and then sank, and the watcher called down to the men in the qalgi: "*Uivvarasii-ii!* It's going round!" and the shout, from every qalgi roof, crossed Tikigaq.

> *Samaruna said:*
> The sun goes round.
> It's come round from the north.
> It's circled Tikigaq
> all spring and summer.
> Now the sun goes round,
> it touches the Point,
> and goes down through the sea
> on the western horizon.
>
> *Asatchaq:*
> It goes south in the winter,
> to where the whales live.
> Next spring it returns
> with the migrant animals.

When the sun went down and the moon lit the twilight, the men swept up their work and pushed it underneath the benches.

Now the sun had touched the Point, the old men started talking. The old men, who had been sleeping or singing and fixing their drum heads, started to tell stories, and the qalgi rituals started.

Asatchaq:
The old men have their places.
They sit on their benches
in the middle of the qalgi.
The old men sit.
Their work is finished.
They do nothing.

Samaruna:
The old men are frightening.
What they know is powerful:
what they know has qilya and is qilya:
songs and stories gathered
in them over many winters.

If anyone offends old men,
withholds meat and keeps it hidden,
walks past the old men without their permission:
that man may have to wait,
but his punishment comes later:
a hand, a leg or the belly will swell,
his fingers will grow numb
when he fixes his bow string,
the ice will crack,
in fair weather, and maroon him:
in its time, this will come,
because old men have qilya.

Asatchaq:
Their songs travel and attack the body.
Their stories have qilya.
What happened in the past
lives on in stories.
They use this like shamans.
Old men are shamans.

For the old have survived, by skill and luck manipulated
    through lives long enough to validate the knowledge
they inherited from elders who, themselves from elders,
    learned to tackle and survive extreme conditions:
each near-impossibility converted to procedure and tactic:

threading *ways* through sea-ice for their seal and bear meat,
  with the acquisition, on each safe return with meat, of knowledge:
the path of each journey, worked in with the knowledge pattern,
  passed vertically down kin lines, and spread through the qalgis.

What the old men knew and taught were knowledge systems
  which had power, qilya, and exerted qilya:
and these were deployed against energies
  that made life dangerous and unpleasant:

high wind and currents, snow-drift, blizzards,
  rivers impassable or too shallow to navigate,
high seas, winter darkness, summer marsh lands and mosquitoes,
  rough capes, hunting in famine through vast empty tundra,
walking tangled shifting sea-ice, kayaking through young mush,
  dragging animals up-wind over sea-ice through the darkness,
hunting polar bear and brown bear, great souls, dangerous,
  whose skins torn, meat ingested, shades placated,
demanded expeditions, expiation, and their repetition:

these – the totality, at each angle preying on the hunter's body,
  assaulting what the mind deflected or was bent to –
were daily confronted by Tikigaq hunters;
  and generated, by their opposition, means, skill and qilya:
an elaborated system, matching, formal counter-construct
  transmitted by example and in stories.

On account of what they'd known and told, and therefore given,
  the ancestors were complete and perfect:
and the living, who inherited the forebears' name souls,
  were a partial incarnation of these namesakes.

But the living were faced daily with ordeals
  revealing human imperfection,
and so they faltered, they thought, badly.
  Divided between present and ancestral selves,
the discord made the makeshift of the present seem a failure,
  and this bound them closer to the elders' precepts.

Halfway towards ancestral status, their hunting finished,
  with a knowledge of the dead that they alone remembered,
the elders, too, were sacred:
  and the stories they recited every autumn formed a web that
        united past and present,
  and sacralised the present before winter started.

So in autumn, the old men started to tell stories.
    All that evening, when the sun touched the Point,
and next day, and the nights and days that followed,
    they told Tikigaq's stories,
tying everyone who had been out all summer
    along sea coasts and inland among strangers,
to the narratives, precisely recollected,
    that united them with all Tikigaq people.

Now the past returned. It *came round* to the present
    in the *things that had been said*, their genealogies and actions,
drawing lines from *back then* closer, so the kin ties
    between namesakes and their forebears reached the present
        unbroken.

All Tikigaq stories lay in two distinct strata, distinguished from each
other by both time and content. Close to *now*, like the bones that lay
in nuna, were the chronicles of recent forebears. These were true. They
were histories: *the things that were said of them*: lives of ancestors, their
names and genealogies, worked into each narrative.

Then there were the myths and legends, and archaic shaman sagas.
These came from back-then: *taimmani*; no less true, the old men said, but
because of their remoteness and their shamanistic content, separate.

As though to invoke the forebears' presence, *invite them* to the
qalgi, the old men opened with the stories of the recent generations:
great-great-grandparents' histories and people who came after. As they
remembered, so they told them. They said:

    Which families lived and struggled in those ruined iglus,
        which men set up the jaw-bones of each qalgi.
    They told how *that* family of five brothers lived together
        in connected iglus at the west end of Tikigaq,
    how their aana was a woman hunter:
        she killed seals like a man and sewed their noses to her parka.
    How these brothers feuded with their neighbours,
        killed too many people and were exiled from the village:
    while two younger men, whose partnership went out of balance,
    pulled back from their quarrel and ate meat together.
    "This was where the shaman Suuyuk built his iglu.
        He was murdered at Uivvaq.
    He had tried to keep the whales from Tikigaq."
        "Kiasik, the wrestler, fought a stranger on the floorboards of
            this qalgi."

"That was the summer Pauluagana shot a large bull caribou,
    and was cutting out the arrow, when he met a Siberian,
right there on Qipaluaq. The man tried to kill him.
    You can still see the grave that Pauluagana dug him."

"Kakianaq's wife. She was Pauluagana's daughter.
    She became a shaman when the singing people took her.
They invited her. She went up there, beyond Qunusiq hill.
    She returned in the autumn. She spoke a new language.
Kamik was her daughter. She understood her mother's language."
    "The madness of Aluuraq. It all started on the north side.
His brother snared a duck and Kinaviiraq claimed it."

There were narratives, too, that illustrated ways
    to judge the movement of the ice and currents,
how to predict the wind's direction,
    which way to jump and turn the body and deploy equipment:
the measurement of force, slope, shift and counter-movement,
    how to read the snow, clouds, winter lights and constellations.
And then stories of the great umialiks and the whales they'd taken.
    How qalgi games and quarrels over whale shares turned to
        fighting.

About skinboats swept out by the ice and stranded,
    how lost crews lived with people who wore walrus skins and
        starved them.
About landfalls among strangers on *the other side*,
    who spoke slowly and ate birds and animals large-boned and
        sour-tasting.
Stories of how warriors came north and killed,
    and how parties of men went south from here and took their
        women.
Of trading partnerships with inland people.
    How boats set out with whale meat, seal oil and belukha,
returning with fawnskins, dried fish, beads and copper.
    Of shamans who fought rivals from the high northern rivers,
dismembered their bodies and put them back together,
    chasing off the animals their rivals hunted,
flew as wind through their qalgis and fire round their caches,
    clashing with their souls on the moon and sea-bed.
All these were histories.

Next came stories from distant, remote winters,
    in the time before *this* time, when the world was unfinished.

When coasts were soft, and earth unstable.
　　It was night with no moon, and days without sunlight.
Snow was seal oil, seal oil was caribou fat.
　　People walked on their hands on the hill-tops where the rocks
　　　　　had hardened,
and hunted the animals they heard barking in the darkness.

And people then were animals. Animals were people.
　　They wore each other's masks and parkas.
The Raven Man was man and raven. There were caribou people,
　　ptarmigan and brown-bear women the first shamans married.
And the animals danced.
　　Owl invited lemming, fox visited the wolverine,
wolves and squirrels had their qalgis,
　　and all these *people* danced, and pushed their masks back,
showed their *human faces* in the fur-ruff's centre, and the shift
　　　　　of feathers.

And *people* exchanged gifts and spouses with their animal partners,
　　held games in the qalgi with their cousins and brothers:
and men fought their wives on the iglu floor,
　　were torn apart and eaten,
returned to life and died again, and took other women
　　who were shamans and ate them.
And back then, everything on earth's crust had a song and was song.
　　Rocks, bone, driftwood, excrement and water.
And song was soul thing, soul was its being.
　　And all things, having soul, were alive with their song,
and singing, spoke their being, as the soul and song were.

And animals and people-who-were-animals
　　in back time were magical and died only to come back again.
They weren't the *real people* who came later,
　　who know death and hunger,
and must learn through their shamans
　　who dreamed into back time,
and taught them the rituals the animals exact of them.
Samaruna said:
I belonged to Unasiksikaaq.
That was the name of my father's qalgi.
There were five other houses:
Suagvik . . . Qaniliqpak . . . Qalgiiraq . . . Qagmaqtuuq and
　　Agraqtagvik . . .

There was another.
I've forgotten its name.
The sea destroyed it.

Asatchaq:
The sea washed it away.
That qalgi stood on the north side, by the north beach.
The waves came up one autumn and the qalgi flooded.

Next spring the ice thawed, and the qalgi exploded.
The roof fell in.
Then the sea pulled the walls out.
My father saw it happen.
When he was small he saw it happen.
The wall-planks and floorboards were dragged off by the current.
People tried to save the whale-jaws.
But they lost the bones from the qalgi ceiling.

One of those jaw-bones had already cracked.
When the ceiling-bones crack, then something will happen.
An umialik will die. Or the qalgi will be ruined.
That's what people say.
And he saw the masks and puppets . . .

Samaruna:
Yes, he saw the qalgi masks and puppets.
They were dragged off on the water too.
I remember him telling us.
The masks lay face-down in the water
and the puppets swung their legs.
There were five brothers in that qalgi,
and they tried to save them.
They took out a boat and tried saving the puppets.

Asatchaq:
That was Suluk and his brothers.
All of them were shamans.
They used a song to try to catch their masks and puppets.

Samaruna:
They didn't make it that time.
Next summer Suluk put his nets out at the inlet.
And when he pulled up his net next morning
there with the salmon was an open-jawed whale:

it was one of the puppets.
It had a salmon in its mouth.
Suluk saw this and told me.
And when he tried untangling it the whale swam away.
It swam off south.
Each of those brothers caught a whale next spring.

Asatchaq:
Because they'd tried to save the qalgi puppets.

Samaruna:
It's true. That story is a good one.
When I was small my uncle took me to his qalgi.
He gave me a chopper to help clear the ice.
It was dark and cold there.
When we'd cleared out the ice the men made a new skylight,
and they lit the oil lamps.
It soon got dry in there.

FOUR ANIMAL FABLES

Samaruna said:
When we were children we used to tell each other stories.
When we played in the iglu,
or watched our parents set their fish nets
from the beach or at the inlet,
when we jigged through the Kuukpak river-ice:
when children came together, we told stories.

Asatchaq:
Yes! we sat in a circle with my oldest cousin, Kamik.
And Kamik took a big flat rock. He stood it upright.
"Knock it over!" said the older children.
So the youngest got up and pushed down the rock.
"*Kitta!* Go on!
Stand it up again!" said the older children.

We ran to the middle and set it upright,
"Push it down!" my cousin whispered.
When the rock had fallen, Kamik said:

"*Aggiaq nappaq!*
Aggiaq nappaq!

The rock's broken in two!
It's broken in two!"

Samaruna:
This taught us about stories.
If you tell only one, the story falls over.
The first needs a partner.

Asatchaq (holds a sealskin line):
Here's a story my cousin told.
There's a song in the story.
I'll sing what he taught me.
Here's the string.
I'll tie it in a circle.
I'll make the figures.
They go with the story:

> *Avinnauraq*
> *igalaam sinaani*
> *kiavalukkatauraaqsiruq*
> *kiavalukatauraliami*
> *kataktuq igalaamin*
> *qiagaqsiruq*
> *"Sung-ang-ang-aa!* *
> *Sung-ang-ang-aa!*
> *Tulimaata navipalukkikka!"*

A lemming,
running round and round
the skylight,
round in a circle
fell through the skylight
and started crying:
"Sung-ang-ang-aa!
Sung-ang-ang-aa!
My ribs! My ribs!
I think I've broken them!"

Samaruna laughs:
That must have happened in someone's iglu.
Here's another – from the lemming's qalgi:

---

* Stressed and chanted: / ∪ ∪ /

There was a raven and snowy owl.
They were partners,
and they called each other cousin.
They hunted together.
They liked to eat lemmings.
They hunted on the tundra.
Most of the time they got very little.
Often they ended up with nothing.

Owl and raven were always hungry.
So one day they stopped hunting.
They talked and made plans.

"Let's visit some lemmings.
Let's invite them to a dance."
So they visited the lemming burrows
and called in, saying:

"Go to the qalgi where you hold your dances.
Tell everyone we'll meet you there!
Tell everyone to come and watch us.
We want to dance for you lemming people!"

Asatchaq laughs:
They invited lemmings
to the lemmings' qalgi!

Samaruna:
That's what they told them.
The lemmings had never seen owl and raven dance.
So they said they'd go.
The lemmings were happy.
They went to their qalgi.

When the lemmings were there,
owl and raven followed.
When they got inside the qalgi
they were both very happy
to see all those lemmings.

Asatchaq:
That's what they wanted.

Samaruna:
So the lemmings took their drums

and started singing.
Owl and raven listened for a while.
Then they got on the floor of the lemmings' qalgi.

The lemmings drummed and sang.
Owl and raven started dancing.
They only had one song,
but they danced and repeated it:
Yura-yura Ya-ya!

Yura-yura Ya-ya!
The lemming's shoulderblade is dry!

The more they danced,
the hotter they got.
"After the next one," owl whispered,
"we'll go into action!
You get all you can,
and I'll get what I can."

The lemmings drummed and sang,
and snowy owl and raven danced.
The two of them danced wonderfully.

And the dance was so fine
that the lemmings were enchanted.
Then just before the end,
while the lemmings were still singing,
they flew into action.
Owl ran one way, raven ran the other.
They dived and flew.
They grabbed all they could.

But the lemmings were too fast for them.
They ran down the katak,
and out into the darkness.

Owl and raven looked round them.
The qalgi was empty.
All they had was one lemming between them.
So they cut it in half
and shared the meat between them!
Tavra isua: that's the end of it.

Asatchaq:
Here's another short one.

A lemming and a shrew quarrelled.
Who was the strongest?
"I am!" said the lemming.
"Me!" said shrew.

To settle their quarrel
they decided to play wrist-pull.
When they crossed wrists and pulled,
the skin on lemming's arm tore.

Shrew sang:
> *Avinnam kiasia*
> *makiangiqsuq*
> *Avinnam kiasia*
> *makiangiqsuq.*

> Lemming's shoulderblade
> tears easily!
> Lemming's shoulderblade
> tears easily!

So the shrew won the wrist-pull.
That's the end of it.

Samaruna:
Here's a seagull with a song.
The gull tied a stone round his neck,
and flew across river.
When he reached the far side, the gull said:
"When they start to play games,
I won't be good at anything.
When they play in the autumn,
I won't have a game
I can use to challenge them."
So the gull thought:
"Next I time I cross,
I'll find a bigger rock,
to take across river!"
So he found another rock,
hung it round his neck
and started flying.

Where's the gull's song?
Here! I'll sing it:

Ikpagyumai: igpagyumai.
tirruqtaalingmai: tirruqtaalingmai
tirruqtaa: tirruqtaa:
ikiqmannamumiyaa(yi)
ikiqmannamumiyaa(yi)
agviglugu: agvilugu
aa aliqa yaa aliqa
*aa aliqa yaa aliqa.**

When the gull reached the far side,
he looked for an even bigger rock
to take back with him.
And the gull sang his song again.
But halfway across river,
he fell in the water.
When he landed in the water,
the gull cried:
"Two kayaks are coming!
Two skinboats as well!
They're coming to help me!"

But the kayaks were his feet,
and the skinboats were his wings.
That's what the storyteller said.
The gull thought his feet were kayaks
and his wings were skinboats.
That was the end of the gull and his story.

The Qalgi Games

When the stories were over the older men went home and the young
men started to play ritual games.

First, each qalgi visited a neighbour, and their strongest athletes,
gymnasts and wrestlers challenged one another until the visitor won
every round in a series. Then the hosts walked over to the winners' qalgi
and played until their champion won a series. Then everyone piled in,
and visitors were hosts, and played until *they* had won a series.

This continued all night. Next morning the older men came back and
played, each with his special skill and prowess. They played until the

* Song unintelligible.

visitors won. Then they all went off to the visitors' qalgi and visitors were
hosts and hosts were visitors.

So those who played at home saw the visitors win, and then visited
their hosts till they, as visitors, had won again, and so on, in paired
groups of qalgis, criss-crossing Tikigaq between the six houses, fasting,
awake, for five days and nights of strife and contest.

The games were ordeals of skill, endurance, strength, agility, contor-
tion and balance. Some, like "the gallop" – a long-jump from squatting –
were held in the snow outside the qalgi. But most games, modelled to
the qalgi interior, made use of the qalgi's structure and proportions
and were tensile, miniature, compact, knotted:

> Two men on all fours
> push their heads into the other's chest
> and each tries lifting his opponent.

> Two men clasp their hands,
> and stretch their arms ahead of them.
> They jump around the qalgi through them.

> Jumping on toe-knuckles
> over sticks above the floor planks.
> Kunannauraq always won this!

> A man hangs by the wrist
> from a plank two others carry.
> The man who hangs longest is the winner.

> Two strings with sticks
> are hung above the floor.
> A man lifts himself
> till his hands touch his knee-backs.
> Paulaurana did this eight times.
> No one ever challenged him.

> Some men hold up a board.
> Another crouches on it.
> Jumping from all fours
> he lands on two.

> Sippik used to fix a knife, point up,
> and bend over it backwards
> till his palms reached the floor.

Men run sideways
on the qalgi wall.
The one who runs furthest
is the winner!

They fix a post to the middle of the floor,
and jump at it
hanging with the feet and hands,
and then jump backwards.

Twist your feet round your arms
so the feet are off the floor,
then hop on your hands across the qalgi!

Raised by his hair through the katak,
he's dragged round the oil lamp.
Sometimes another man stands on his body.

Between two whale-floats is a double seal-thong.
The crew save it, and the leather hardens.
Two men stand and whip each other –
hard across the ribs!
When one man gives up, another comes forward.

Quwana fixed a thread of seal-line to a board
and laid the board outside across the skylight.
He sat down and raised himself,
slowly rising:
then hung without falling,
without breaking the seal-line.

A man in Suagvik invented his own game.
He sharpened a walrus tusk
and lay down with his nose on it.
Two men took the bottom of the tusk
and lifted him on it until he was standing.
A man from the other qalgi said,
"Do that with my knife!"
"I'll try," said the first man
– his face already bleeding – "when you have!"
The challenger stepped back,
so the tusk-game man won.
He went home to his qalgi.

They walk: elbows pressed to ribs on the hands;
     walk knees in elbows;
  walk pulling legs behind on knees and chin;
     walk chin off the floor on knees and chest;
  walk on knuckles, legs out, toes hopping behind;
     walk on one foot-and-hand: the other leg
  stretched back off the floor,
       one hand to front ankle.

Whatever the last game, the winning qalgi was overall winner. When one side ran out of challengers and challenges they had to admit they'd lost the series.

While the ancient stories rehearsed myth-time, the games acted out in silent diagram the conflicts in the story symbols: Raven and the uiluaqtaq woman, moon-brother/sun-sister, light against darkness, hunter and animal, the forms of the games evoking the archaic fables in which animals – quarrelsome, competitive and metamorphic – tricked one another, fought, or mated, registered their evolution, confirmed their endurance.

For animals, too, have their feast times and qalgis:
     each kind bound in name-form to its company of spirits:
  societies of "people", living underground, on land, or in the water,
     migrants, at death, moving south to where they've come from,
  again to take bodies, re-enter the cycle.

But whether souls range free, or wear animal meat and outer parkas,
     they sing, race, jump, dance, wrestle, and hold contests,
  inviting fellow species to their ceremonial houses,
     to contrive, where they can, both a welcome and a trouncing.

In the stress and play of qalgi violence –
     tactics abstracted from their paths of impact,
  one story-creature on another –
     the lines of energy were rough and primal:

as though birth-death, tangled in the players' bodies,
     rapped out the percussion – hunting, conflict, sexuality –
  most encounters between beings constitute.

Likewise the winner–loser, host–guest oscillation,
     responsive and in counterpoint between the qalgis,
  maintained balance in their conflicts:
     the stress regulated to maintain an equilibrium,

so winners who won were winners entirely,
while the losers, when they lost, sprang back to become winners.

Thus the games extended across Tikigaq in flexible symmetry,
    like the string figures children and old people wove,
whose mobile patterns likewise enacted animal stories:
    foxes bounding through loops of seal-thong,
ptarmigan snared in complex thickets, caribou constructed
    out of geometric tangles, to collapse in the hands
as the seal-string resolved to the matrix of its circle.

But perhaps above all the games foreshadowed the ascetic vigil of
the whale hunt, when the players would be crewmen and umialiks in
competitive abstention, sleepless and fasting on the sea and sea-ice,
poised each day and daylight night-time for the moment of the whale's
rise and the harpoon strike in which every previous ritual action merges.

After the games the men went home and bathed in urine. They livened
their amulets with birth-stuff or death-things, and then rubbed their
bodies with them.

If a man was injured his amulets would heal him. When everyone
had done this they went back to their qalgis and the women brought
them raw, fermented seal meat. The meat made them sleepy. They slept
in their qalgis.

Samaruna:
I forgot. While the men are in their qalgis,
their wives stay home.
They stop work while the men play.
The women don't sew.
They don't cut meat or skins or sinew.
If they work in their iglus,
their husbands will be injured.

Asatchaq:
It's the same at whaling.
While the men are on the sea-ice,
the women stay home.
They sit in their iglus.
They do nothing.

Samaruna:
The sun goes down and the moon takes over.
While the old men tell stories,

the young ice sets along the beaches.
While they play in the qalgi,
the pack-ice approaches.

Asatchaq:
When the pack-ice has come,
the men can go hunting.

Samaruna:
But the last game is next spring.
The last game is the whale hunt.
Whoever gets the first whale is the winner.

Asatchaq:
The qalgi whose umialik takes the first whale wins.
But the qalgi games last five days.
Like shamans who take five days in trance-sleep,
when their souls are travelling.

Samaruna:
Five days, five nights.
Shamans bound with seal-line.
Crouched in darkness. Unborn.
Soul-death. Soul-birth.

Asatchaq:
No one must wake them.

Yugaq: The Amulet Dances

The games led into a series of dances that continued at intervals through the autumn.

The dances were accompanied by whale-lung membrane drums whose circular wooden frames were struck from below. The sharp beat of the stick was thus harmonically enveloped in the deeper resonance of vibrating drum skins. Above the two-beat of percussion the drummers sang in a high register of syncopated half-tone phrases.

There were songs for all occasions, which the magical nature of words and melody made potent. Ritual songs were powerful both on account of the hypnotic vibrational impact of repeated exclamation and also for their origins.

Many songs had supernatural origin: they were learned in trance from spirits or animals, composed in dreams, inherited from forebears, transmitted by shamans who had realised them in ancient or strange languages.

Once a song was known and ingested it became part of the body. Sometimes the recipient took saliva from the singer's mouth to ensure the transfer of linguistic reality. The older a song, the more powerful its shamanistic life. But all these songs had spiritual validity provided they were performed word- and note-perfect in the right context. A song which was used where it had no place or ritual function was drained of virtue.

Many songs were also carefully and consciously composed to celebrate life events, conflicts, animals and places. These could be magical too, and become over time part of qalgi repertoire.

And just as songs were usually allusive and cryptic, often deliberately archaic or arcane in diction – sometimes a mere *aya-ya-ya* refrain set to a melodic line, or a scatter of fragmented ambiguities whose narrative sense was too well known to require explanation – so many dances traced familiar lore in abstract, compressed choreography.

Everyone had an inherited dance, and most people knew the songs that went with them. When a man took the qalgi floor, wearing his mittens with their clinking fawn's-hoof slices to help summon or appease the spirits, the drummers automatically, but with tentative and slightly absent strokes, inducted the rhythm of the dance he called for.

As the singers started the dancer swayed, stirred vaguely, described a few loose circles with his arms and gazed in front of him. Then the tempo gradually increased, the volume rose and the dancer, as though reluctant, ill at ease, perhaps even slightly bored, engaged a little further, though still sketching his movements to eliminate himself as far as possible from the dance pattern he had inherited or invented.

But the point soon arrived where song and drum reached an intensity that the performer must follow. This, in other rituals, was the path the shaman entered, dancing to exhaustion till he "died", allowing one of the souls inhabiting all humans to depart and range the mythic cosmos. The shaman lay in trance, sometimes bound with rope in foetal posture, until the freed soul returned from its mystical journey.

Whereas shamanistic dancing had this special, extreme purpose, the qalgi dance was part of communal activity and the performance must unfold until its pattern was completed.

The form of the dance extended beyond the particularities of movement to a network of social and metaphysical connections: between dancer and audience, between kinsmen and namesakes who danced to each other, between host and guest qalgis, and between the living who danced and the ancestors whose gestures were enacted.

The first autumn dances also conjured the animals. Everyone was connected with one or more animals through amulets given at birth by a spiritual guardian from another qalgi.

According to the guardian's choice people carried wolf's teeth, foxtails, owl-, ptarmigan- and squirrel-skins, effigies of whales and walrus, eagles' heads and ravenskins. They wore these constantly: hanging them on cords round their necks, or on belts, in bags, or sewn to the outside of their parkas.

When they were sick people chewed their amulets to activate them with saliva, rubbed the amulet on birth- or death-stuff to generate still further power, used the amulet to massage their bodies and called on the animal spirit to help them.

The shaman's connections were still more intimate. He had visited the spirit homes of certain animals, or slept with an amulet bride in a dream and been torn up and eaten. Or he had learned seal, caribou or polar-bear language, or seen an animal reveal the human face of its inua that lay beneath the *mask* of its species.

The shaman carried amulets of animals which had taught him their lore in these visions. And when he was called on to perform in the qalgi, he could choose to transform to this amulet familiar.

> Then he'd slip
> into his other self and vanish through the katak:
>   bear claws, loon's bill or wolftail flashing
> to confound the audience and signify his metamorphosis.

After the games the losers visited the winners' qalgi. They came up through the entrance-hole bearing spits full of meat held aloft and bundles of sinew and sealskin boot soles as gifts for the old people.

> Setting the meat in the middle of the qalgi,
>   they cried, "We'll return!"
> The hosts reached for their meat, and answered with a roar
>   as the visitors withdrew.

Later that day, painted, in new skins, in half-masks, they returned with their families. With gifts for namesakes, kinsfolk and guardians, they came up in twos. When the qalgi was full they climbed up on to the roof and looked down through the skylight.

> The visitors came dressed as their amulet animals.
>   They came to dance in amulet costumes:

bear's nose and a loon's head –
    polar bears and loons are both good divers,
their amulets work well together –
    wolf-head, wolfskin ruff and wolftail,
wolverine, jaws open and claws hanging,
    half one skin, half another, half snowy owl, half squirrel,

half fur outside, half turned-out leather,
    half black and ochre faces,
half the face bare to signify the double amulet,
    dancing for their guardians and namesakes.

And the dancers cry in their amulet voices,
    in the voices of their helping animals:
brown bear, red fox, peregrine and golden eagle,
    raven, gull and marmot, grebe and lemming,
double being, dancing to their doubles,
    song and drum beat, shouting through the katak,
        "Ui! Ui!
Ui! Ui!"

dancing to their living namesakes,
    the dead namesakes' dances:
through the animals and souls
    they killed and worshipped.

Since the tempo of song has quickened, the dancer's movements grow more muscular and sharply angled. The calm of the first patterns, the vague eyes and drifting feet, transform to a rhythmically percussive flood of gestures, diagramming stories, lives and visions.

The hands harpoon, the arms paddle kayaks,
    the dancer hunts, he triumphs, opening his chest, lets fly with
        arrows.
Stamping with the drums, the right foot shakes the qalgi
    and the high arms cross, the open hands
flex, curve, invite, control, placate, defend, invoke,
    conjure the dance signs that the maker jointed.

Whether it is character that flows
    through the weaving-without-person
that the dancer created with his first design,
    or the force of dance-form
that drives hands, voice, arms and feet,

it's uncertain who is dancing there:
man, spirit, ancestor or some compound of these,
    while from the dancer's centre the amulets fly outwards,
tails, beaks, teeth and feathers flung and shaking,
    till the spirits approach and the dance is spirit.

The dancer is a loon, he juts his neck, retracts, recoils,
    his hard eye flicks, and his half-open mouth,
unhuman with dance cry, reveals his own shadow
    and the spirit of the teaching animal.

As the souls in the dance-joints loosen and stream free,[*]
    the bird's-neck rhythm of his nodding from a straight trunk
jerks the chin through regulated spasms;
    hands and feathers mask and unmask,
and the dancer's face disc, opening to show its forebears,
    merges and dissolves with them.

"That dance was *him!*"
    The elders who have seen the forebears know its antecedent.
Woven into compound being
    and played on a screen
the drum has stretched across the present,
    the song ends abruptly and the dancer pauses.
Poised on one foot, he balances in silence,
    till the next masked dancer leaps up through the katak.

Silence: Trading

After the dancing the men stayed in their qalgis and continued to work on their equipment. The men used this interlude for inter-qalgi trading.

At first each deal was anonymous and conducted through agents. Two agents of the principal sat outside a rival qalgi and displayed wooden models, strung on rawhide, of trade goods a colleague in their qalgi had to offer.

The men came out and inspected the carvings. If someone was interested he tied a model of goods offered in exchange to the agents' string.

The two agents returned to their qalgi and presented the composite string to their principal. If the trader agreed to the transaction he visited the other qalgi and completed his business.

---

* These are souls that live in the joints of animals and some humans.

Samaruna:
That's how we made new partnerships.
Old partners trade too.
When I have skins or seal oil
I send a gift to my partner's qalgi
and ask what I want from him.

Asatchaq:
Partners can ask anything.
A skinboat even.
If he's asked,
he has to send it.

Samaruna:
There once was a man in Suagvik qalgi.
He asked his partner
for the smell of flesh,
with the smell of sawn wood.

Asatchaq:
His partner sawed his own leg off.
He sent it to the man who'd asked for it.

Between Yugaq and the Sitting

The qalgis are halfway through their autumn rituals. The men sleep in their qalgis, or go home to their families. The shamans and umialiks prepare for the Sitting: a new group of rituals invoking the animals and focused on next season's whale hunt.

In contrast to the dances and the games of Yugaq the Sitting starts quietly. All the qalgis fall silent. The umialiks are taboo. They walk slowly, sit in contemplation; they are mystical and dangerous.

Waterpots, mittens and feeding the children

Some time in the autumn, before the sea-ice formed, each umialik couple would stand at the tip of the Point and pour fresh water on a wave. This would bring whales to Tikigaq next spring, for whales' souls are thirsty and want freshwater.

Later in the autumn, when mush-ice formed along the beaches, male umialiks visited carvers who made *qattaqs* for the women. Umialik wives would use these pots next spring. When their husbands caught whales the women would offer fresh water to the whales' souls.

The construction of the pot filled several days and nights. When the shape had been cut, but still not bent round, the craftsman tied the wood and the shavings in a bundle and went with his umialik to dip it in sea-water. A special song accompanied this ritual.

Next the umialik took the pot home and left it in the iglu passage. A few days later he took the pot to the qalgi passage. Finally the pot was brought home and hung above the oil lamp.

Next morning the craftsman came to bend the wood and stitch it with baleen. He fitted a bottom and a handle to the pot and strung beads to each join. A small whale, carved in ivory or bone, was hung inside from a thong.

Finally the owner fixed two feathers to the qattaq. These would help lift their pots to the moon, for Alinnaq, the spirit of the moon, liked water too. The feathers were from birds in the creation story. They helped raise the pot to Alinnaq's iglu: raven one side, peregrine the other. These feathers – opposite, together – gave wings to the qattaq.

While the pot was being made the woman umialik visited an older woman to order some mittens to carry the pot with. The mittens were shaped like bowhead whales, sewn in darkened and bleached sealskin to imitate maktak.

If the woman and her husband were successful and caught a whale the following spring, she'd return for a new pair of mittens. The same happened with the pot. If the two were successful they chose the same carver.

When all the women had finished their sewing the next stage of the rituals started.

The first thing the umialiks did was call the children. This was both a joke and an initiation. The children were told they'd get *quluguluguqs*. But they didn't understand the word. The children thought it meant they'd be given stuck-together bits of fish as presents.

"Get a piece of whale fat," their parents told them. "Put it on a stick and go to the qalgi. You'll see lots of *quluguluguq!*"

While the children found their bits of blubber the qalgis were prepared for their return. At the back of the house there was a hollow in the floor where the men kept masks, puppets, figurines of ancestors and shamans, miniature skinboats and other ritual carvings. These were the *quluguluguqs*. Soon, for the Sitting, they'd be hung from the qalgi ceiling.

The men took all the carvings and piled them in a hollow in the middle of the qalgi, where the meat was cut up. When the children came in they looked for their fish, and saw the carvings. Instead of getting gifts of food the children were told to put their whale fat in another hole, beneath the qalgi oil lamp. This would feed the lamp for the coming ritual. Thus the children fed the lamps with whale fat.

Next day the umialiks went to their caches to fetch meat for the children. The children still kept their wooden spits, and ran round the village to each umialik's iglu. Climbing the roof they lowered their spits though the iglu skylight, while the umialiks stood inside and skewered meat on the spits until they were full.

The umialiks then feasted their skinboat crews. First the crews came and helped cut maktak into strips. Each strip had to be measured against the umialik woman. If the woman was tall the strip of maktak must be long. If she was short the whaleskin was cut as short as she was. Each length was then chopped and taken to the qalgi and piled into the meat-carving hollow. In their black and white mittens the women gave chunks of black and white maktak to each of the crewmen.

Next day the umialiks put on new clothes and went to their qalgis. While the women took their pots and stood in the passage the men went inside to wait on their benches.

Then the other qalgi members came.
    They all came in, except for one shaman.
This shaman stayed home until he was summoned.
    When the qalgi messenger called down through his skylight,
"*Qamma pigaatin:* You're wanted!"
    the shaman took his parka off,
and his wife drew whale flukes on his chest with lamp soot.

Then the shaman chose a helper,
    and they walked out to the south shore.
The shaman took his drum; his helper took a knife and chopper.
    When the two men reached the first crack in the new young ice,
the shaman drummed and started singing.
    While he drummed the shaman's assistant cut a piece of sea-ice,
and he took his knife and carved an ice-whale for the qalgi.

The shaman never stopped. He drummed and sang.
    And when the shaman was in trance,
the man who was carving saw flukes from a whale's tail,
    he saw whale flukes growing from the shaman's mouth.

They walked back to the village.
    They approached the qalgi.
The shaman's assistant went in first.

He put his ice-whale by the katak.
Then the shaman went in.
   He had been waiting in the passage.
And he leapt up from the passage:
   his head rose in the katak.

The women were inside now. The women had their qattaqs.
   And when they saw the shaman's head rise,
when the umialik women saw his whale flukes,
   when he raised his whale flukes through the katak,
the women gave him water.
   They splashed water on him from their qattaqs.

Every time the shaman came up through the katak,
   one of the women gave him water.
The shaman drank and dived back,
   whale flukes rising and diving through the katak.
The whale flukes vanished at the final qattaq,
   The shaman went home.
The ice-whale was left between the lamp and katak.
   That whale never melted.

Sacred water rituals

One mile east of the village, between the inlet and the lagoon, lay a freshwater pond called Umigraagvik. Here, when the shamans-who'd-been-whales had drunk their water, the umialiks walked to cut ice-blocks to make qalgi passage skylights.

After the Sitting the ice-skylights would be chopped up and given to the woman umialiks. The women would keep the pond-ice for their pots. That winter they'd splash water on the moon. Next spring they'd give their whales a drink of water.

Umigraagvik pond was sacred to the women because a supernatural whale had been created there. The whale had been made from the vaginal blood of a uiluaqtaq:

Asatchaq said:
It started with a woman who refused to take a husband.
She was a uiluaqtaq: a woman who won't marry.
Because of this the men in her father's qalgi punished her.
They hung a caribou-skin in the qalgi,
and behind it they raped her.

The last man was Aaliaq. He had a big penis.
Aaliaq's penis made the uiluaqtaq bleed.

While all this happened the father stood on the qalgi roof
and called through the skylight:
"Daughter! when they've finished,
wipe yourself with the hem of your parka!"
The woman went home,
and her father cut the hem of her bloodstained parka.
Next spring, the man cut the skin again and sewed it.
When he'd finished, the bloodstained skin was a little whale.
The man left his iglu, and walked to Umigraagvik.
The man had a song.
He sang it as he put the skin-whale into Umigraagvik:

> *Allamun pisaanak!*
> *Allamun pisaanak!*
> Don't go to other boats!
> Just go to Aaliaq's!

The skin came to life. It was a little whale.
It dived and then rose. But before it grew too big,
the man moved it over to Ipiutak.
When the whale dived and rose again,
he pulled it from the water.
He rolled it down the north beach and pushed it in the water.
The whale started swimming.
It swam along the north side.
And when the men saw it they launched their skinboats.
The whale swam ahead.
But when the boat-crews saw it was a magic whale
they turned back to the village.
Only Aaliaq continued.
And when he was close enough he harpooned it.
Aaliaq struck the whale the uiluaqtaq's father made.
But instead of diving with the whale-float,
the whale turned round, and smashed the skinboat.
Aaliaq was drowned.
The uiluaqtaq's father was revenged on him.
That's why people visit Umigraagvik.
Someone made a whale there with a uiluaqtaq's bloodstained parka.

The Umialiks Walk to Umigraagvik

The morning after the shaman had grown whale flukes the male umialiks, caped with peregrine falcon- and ravenskins, gathered the young men and orphans from their qalgi and walked to Umigraagvik, dragging a boat-sled with small bits of meat that were strung on a seal-line.

When they got there the young men took knives and choppers and cut a disc of ice from Umigraagvik. While the shamans drummed the umialiks put meat on the ice-disc and the young men ate. Then each umialik took a small piece of whaleskin and, throwing it inland, away from the sea, said, "I'm going to kill a whale!" and dropped a piece of meat through the ice-hole.

Then they walked to the lagoon and fed the rest of the meat to ancestors' spirits. The umialiks followed the sled home, singing, and laid the ice-disc, as a special skylight, on the qalgi passage. Carrying harpoons they went into the qalgi and sat down quietly.

The women stood outside on the roof. They took their qattaqs and poured water on the ice-disc. Then they went home and put their pots and mittens by the oil lamp.

Sitting

The first day

When they came back from the pond the umialiks went home to their iglus and the young men, boys and orphans slept in the qalgis.

Early next morning the umialiks hurried back with gifts. They competed to come early to show they were generous. As they arrived they climbed the qalgi roof and tapped the skylight. The boys woke up and ran outside to get the meat the umialiks had brought them.

When the qalgi was empty the men went in. They entered quietly. No one dragged his feet or stamped. The younger umialiks went to their benches. Some sat on the land side and faced towards the sea. Some sat facing inland, on the seaward side. One bench-place opposite the katak was kept for a shaman. The oldest umialiks sat to each side of him.

Then the umialik women entered. They had waited in the passage with their pots and mittens. When the men were ready the women joined them. The women wore their belts and parkas loose. Loose clothes made them sleepy, so the whales next season would be quiet and sleepy.

Asatchaq said:
Those women umialiks wear headbands made of wolfskin.
They've sewn eagle feathers to their parkas.

Samaruna:
The wolf soul
and the whale are partners.
Umialik women
bring the wolf's soul
to the qalgi.

Umialik women
hunt whales with their husbands,
Back then, in the stories,
there were whale-hunting eagles . . .

Asatchaq:
There was a girl, they say,
who was an eagle.
She kept her parka
in the iglu passage.
When her brother was hungry,
that girl put her parka on,
and changed into an eagle.

She flew out to sea,
she flew down on whales.
When she came home,
she always brought a whale with her.
That girl taught her brother
to fly in her parka.

Samaruna:
One kind of whale she told him not to touch
was a whale that blew red spray.
That story's a long one . . .

Now the umialiks were in taboo. They moved slowly. They were grave.
The village was silent. No one talked to the umialiks. No one sang or
worked on equipment.

Four days the umialiks sat. They thought about the whales they would
catch. They thought, and they saw them. It was frightening and sacred.

And now the umialiks told their families to open their caches. "Feed
the old people, poor people and orphans!" The umialiks were generous.
Their meat stores were opened. The more they gave, the more whales
would come and lend their bodies.

And now the shamans chose what umialiks could eat.
    Each umialik listened to his shaman.
Some were told to eat whale's back, flipper, waist or belly.
    Some to eat only skin and blubber.
Others were forbidden to eat whale,
    but ate bear meat or seal.
Each umialik was told what to eat,
    so the souls in the meat would agree with his amulets.

Samaruna said:
Because animals know what we do in Tikigaq.
They know the umialiks.
If umialiks are generous,
the whales will be generous.

On their way to Tikigaq,
before they get here, the whales always stop.
And they talk to each other.

"Those who feed the poor and old, we'll go to.
We'll give them our meat,
we'll lend them our parkas.

But umialiks who hoard food,
who keep whale meat back for themselves:
they won't catch us.
We'll avoid them."

That's how the whale thinks.

Before they had walked to Umigraagvik pond someone in each qalgi had been chosen to grind chalk from a cliff near the village and make white paint with it.

On the first day of the Sitting the umialiks used the paint to decorate the whale-jaws in the qalgi walls. Removing their parkas, each umialik took a feather that worked well with his amulets. In turn they then dipped the feather in the paint and drew on the whale-jaw.

They drew scenes from the whale hunt: men in skinboats, whales rising and blowing, harpooners striking, harpooned whales with drag-floats trailing, the spring whale festival, miraculous harpoonings.

One umialik always drew a man with his hands outstretched to stop a whale escaping. This was Atchuuraq: a poor boy of legend who'd transformed to a walrus.

The second day

When they'd finished painting the umialiks turned to the carvings and puppets they would use for the next four days of Sitting.

Each qalgi owned two groups of these sacred objects. The first were the quluguluguqs they had tricked the children with. These were kept in their hollow in the qalgi floor and produced each year when the children visited.

The second group was called puguq. These were carved by umialiks when the qalgis opened and then burned at the end of the autumn rituals.

The two groups of carvings were somewhat like the two classes of story. The quluguluguqs were mythic effigies: generations old, rich with symbolic association. Each figurine had a story that went with it. These stories were told at the end of the rituals.

The puguqs, carved each autumn, portrayed recent ancestors or wonderful exploits of qalgi members. Hunters also carved puguqs of the animals they wanted.

So, after the children had left the qalgi, the men washed the carvings. Then, accompanied by special songs, the figurines were hung on sealskin strings from the qalgi ceiling. These were some of the sacred carvings.

QULUGULUGUQS

Daylight beginning

The first is the *Daylight beginning* board.
　　It stretches across the qalgi wall.
The board is painted
　　in black and white sections:
daylight in white paint,
　　darkness in soot bands.
There are white spots on black bands,
　　black spots on white.
This is daylight and darkness.
　　Daylight beginning!

Whale, raven and skinboats

A whale, two skinboats and a raven
　　hang on strings.
The skinboats chase the whale!
　　Harpooners strike!
The raven dives!
　　The raven steals blubber!
Whale and Raven! Help us catch Whales!

Kayak and whale, and Tatqiavluk's mask

Here's the kayak and whale.
　　The whale rises and blows!
The kayaker strikes!
　　It's poor boy Tatqiavluk!

He was travelling by kayak.
　　Down by Imnat after whaling.
A whale rose near him.
　　Poor boy was alone,
with a seal-spear, in his kayak.
　　He struck! He sang!
Uivvaluk! Uivvaluk!
　　"Round! Round! Round!
The whale-float goes round!"

"Tatqiavluk is umialik now!"
　　When he was old he never left the oil lamp.

His mask has eyes.
  The ears have pendants.
The men keep it warm by the qalgi oil lamp
  Tatqiavluk! Help me get a whale!

Atchuuraq: walrus shaman

The round head of Atchuuraq
  has walrus tusks.
Poor boy mocked shamans.
  He roared like those who roar like walrus.
One night he grew tusks.
  He ran out crying.
"One of those shamans must have got me!"
  "He's been given what he wanted!"
He slept in the qalgi with the other orphans.
  When he woke up, Atchuuraq was happy.
He dived through the katak.
  Everyone saw his walrus flippers going.
Atchuuraq! spread your hands!
  Stop whales escaping!

Caribou Soul (Inua) Mask

There's a human face in the caribou forehead.
  When the caribou butted its skin-mask on the tundra,
the mask slid up; it showed its inua.
  The caribou said:
"I want to change heads with you!"
  The shaman, changing, gazed in terror.
Now caribou souls have human faces.
  Caribou, caribou! help us live properly!

PUGUQS

Umialik and whale

The umialik points his finger.
  A black whale rises.
The umialik wears gut,
  with a quill-tube in it.
The qalgi men blow.
  His parka's breathing!

The black whale rises!
The pointing umialik's breathing, breathing!

Umigluk's vision

He ran along the south beach to the village,
　　and the skinboat circled the air above him.
The skinboat umialik had one eye in his forehead.
　　He shook the copper trinkets on his mittens.
Spirit of Umigluk: we see your vision!

The shaman Asatchaq in flight to Siberia

He lay in the qalgi.
　　They bound him with seal-line.
His rival, "Hand", flew up,
　　with one leg bent, to meet him.
Asatchaq! namesake! we shall both continue!

Brown bear spirit helper

My father hung from Imnat.
　　Brown bear pulled him upward: up with his inwards.
Spirit friend: our souls are connected!

Animal puguqs

All the animals hang there.
　　When the women bring meat,
they raise it to their husbands' drawings.
　　The women umialiks feed the images.
Animals, animals! we travel to fetch you!

The third day

The third day of Sitting was in halves, twos, contrasts, joining, alternation.

Umialiks made white deerskin half-masks, which they'd painted in soot with scenes from whaling. They sat together quietly, hosts on their benches, guests in the middle.

The hosts joined hands. They leaned towards the sea, then slowly swayed towards the mainland. They sang in a murmur, swaying faster, singing louder, until, giddy with rhythm, the qalgi roared, and jabbed hands

seaward!
> to the Point!
and jabbed hands
> to the *mainland!*

Samaruna:
Umialik men danced.
And then the hosts said:
"We've finished!
Go back to your qalgi!"
But the visitors refused.
They stayed to watch the skinboat puppets:
pointing, breathing, paddling, singing!

Asatchaq:
They watched.
Then they left to begin their own dances.
And a woman umialik gave the children maktak.
As the last child went out, she took her pot,
and poured water on him through the katak.

On the third day of the Sitting (Suluk, Day of Feathers) hosts and
qalgi visitors came in wearing headbands stuck with feathers. There was
silence in the qalgi: hosts on their benches, guests round the katak and
standing behind them.

The guests bowed their heads. The hosts started singing. Then,
nodding and swaying, the guests cried out in the voices of their amulet
animals:

Seals barked from the sea-ice.
> Walrus roared among the ice-floes.
Foxtails sewn to parkas yapped by Pitmigiak river.
> Wolf snouts, running along Tungaak, howled.
Brown bear at Imnat hummed and grunted.
> Ptarmigan croaked and little *sii-sr-iik* wheezed and chattered.
Outside their burrows, on the flanks of Amaqtusuk, marmot
> whistled.
> Polar bear snored in pressure-ridge snow-caves.
Short-eared owl's voice – "it flies soundless" –
> grated through the midnight summer.
Kek-kek-kek! cried Peregrine above the willows.
> Gulls and kittiwakes wept round their ledges.

A-haa-liq! (Old Squaw) on the melt ponds hiccuped its three
    syllables.
  Loons on the river laughed and mated.
Snow geese clanging *qang-uaq! qang-uaq!* splashed down on
    the marshes.
  The black whale, in effigies of chert and ivory,
breath exploding in the water – *Aappah! Aah-paah!* –
    drummed on the membrane of the qalgi chanting.

Samaruna:
When the animals had spoken,
the guests raised their heads,
and showed their faces.

Asatchaq:
The animals had gathered.
Now they were *people*,
they joined the singing.

Each qalgi owned a wooden top called *qipsuk*, which had down from an
eagle's breast fixed to its edges. The top was spun to divine the qalgi's
future. When the people gathered for the qipsuk show their lives were in
the hands of the qipsuk spinner and the qipsuk's spinning.

  The people crowded round the spinner and the old men sitting on
their benches drummed.

  The spinner knelt on one knee in the centre of the qalgi and wound
sinew round qipsuk. Squatting by the top the spinner danced, on one
knee, four dances, to bring life to qipsuk. At the climax of the drumming
the dancer whipped away the sinew and set the top spinning.

Asatchaq:
Spinning shows the qalgi what will happen.
The hand of the spinner holds its future.
If the top spins fast, and the eagle-down flies,
there'll be whales for that qalgi,
and life for its members.

Samaruna:
Qipsuk looks inside.
It sees what will happen.
But if the sinew breaks,
or the eagle-down won't fly,
There'll be death in that qalgi.

The fourth day

The last day of Sitting was called *day for calling: day for killing*. When the qalgi had assembled, and had sung for some hours, the singers called out the names of each umialik.

> *Samaruna:*
> They called Suluk, and he answered:
> "I want to kill a whale! Right now!"
> They called
> Kunuyaq and he said:
> "I want to kill a whale! Right now!"
>
> *Asatchaq:*
> They called Sivvik and she answered:
> "I want to kill a whale! Right now!"
> They called Niguvana and she answered:
> "I want to kill a whale! Right now!"

When all the umialiks had answered the singers, the rest of the qalgi called out what they wanted:

> "I want caribou this autumn!"
>   "I want seals this winter!"
> "I want sons and daughters!"
>   "I want long life!"
> "I want polar bear and ugruk!"
>   "I want fox- and wolfskins!"

Finally they killed the carvings. To the rhythm of drumming, the elders told the story of each hanging figure. When a story was finished the men took spears and struck the carvings.

> *Samaruna:*
> Umialiks speared the whales they'd hung.
> They sang what they'd sing at next season's whale hunt.
>
> *Asatchaq:*
> This was the last thing they did at the Sitting.

They Burn the Hangings: Qalgi Carnival

Next day, at a "burning place" outside their qalgis, the men took a whale made of baleen shavings and lit a fire inside the whale's mouth. Then, one by one, they burned their new carved animals.

Samaruna:
They'd invited the animals into the qalgi.
They'd brought them alive with their dances and singing.
Now they let their souls go.
Now they send their souls back to their countries.

Asatchaq:
Because animals that die at sea are thirsty,
women pour water on their burning images.
Because animals from inland are hungry for fat,
women drop seal oil on their burning figures.

Samaruna:
The fires burn out.
Women pour fresh water on the ashes.

Asatchaq:
The souls of the carvings have left Tikigaq.
The people return to their iglus and qalgis.

After they had burned the sacred carvings,
    the village erupted in carnival festivity.
Umialik men swapped their clothes with women,
    others wore ragged, inside-out and upside-down costumes.
Dressed to shock, for pranks and mummery,
    the masqueraders crowded back into their qalgis.
Slapstick dances pantomimed the mythic archetypes
    (grandma-as-husband foisted on the woman-who-won't-marry!)
while dancers grabbed kisses from their namesakes' spouses,
    and received, in return, a bantering, erotic punishment.
There were four days' rest.
    Then the qalgis were re-opened and carnival repeated.
This let go the spirits of the ancient hangings.
    Their souls fled the qalgis. The rituals were over.

Next morning, in new boots and parkas,
    umialiks walked to nuvuk* with their spouses.
The village lay behind them. The qalgis were silent.
    They stood at the Point, between village and sea-ice.
All day, they stood on the frozen gravel,
    watching the young sea-ice, talking quietly, doing nothing.

* The tip of the Point.

WINTER

Five months of winter followed the rituals. Except for occasional shamanic séances the qalgis were closed until the next autumn.

Tikigaq now focused on the daily seal hunt. Carrying harpoons and dragging small sleds, men left their iglus every morning in the dark or the twilight and walked out on the ice in search of breathing holes or open water.

There was competition for space on the safer, more productive south side. But for miles all round the Point, in the hours of light and the afternoon dusk, the ice was studded with the forms of men waiting at breathing holes or open channels.

To travel on the sea around Tikigaq in winter, every hunter had to understand the movements, forms and sounds of the ice as they changed with the wind and the powerful current.

In autumn the inshore ice is too thin to support the body but too dense for kayaking. As the young ice deepens and is joined by the polar ice-pack that drifts south in the autumn, vast fields of layered old and young ice meet, heap, buckle, separate, break up and re-form in a maze of unstable plains and piles of rubble.

Prevailing north and south winds alternate throughout the winter; the current sweeps north; the ice moves in and out, spins round, pushes up hills and ridges under constant pressure. This movement presented a deadly challenge. But without shifts in the ice there would be no open water and no seal hunt.

Most Tikigaq subsistence involved risk and daring, but where sea-ice was concerned young men were always guided by older hunters. It took years before a man could read the ice, wind and current well enough to travel independently.

But the most knowledgeable hunter could always be cut off by a crack that could strand him on an ice-floe or the far side of an open channel. With luck and intelligence, many hunters worked their way to shore after days, even weeks, of terrible exposure; oral tradition abounded in their survival stories. Others made landfalls in neighbouring Alaskan territory. On rare occasions hunters drifted to Siberia. Many perished of exposure.

A sea-ice hunter's life was short and arduous. Most men were worn out

by the age of 40. And winter's routine was often tedious. A diet of seal
was varied only by limited stores of whale and caribou laid down the
previous spring and summer.

Polar bear made a welcome change in mid- to late winter. Some men
hunted in groups, but not with dogs. And the labour of a single-handed
kill, far out on the pack-ice, butchering the animal and dragging home
its skin full of meat over rough ice in the dark against the wind, is
inconceivable.

But polar bear meat was essential when seals were scarce. The skins
made boot-tops, mittens, parka ruffs and blankets; men and women
prized their snouts and teeth as amulets. And few became umialiks
until they had swollen their wealth and status by polar-bear hunting.

Cold and darkness, and tensions between clans and rival shamans,
always threatened and often lethally. But in spite of all this Tikigaq people
saw their land, their village and their animals as wonderful and varied.

Winter was also lit from within by a family life that was joyous and
peaceful. Caring for the elders, adoring their children, extended families
took endless pleasure in their own and others' company. Besides, there
were hundreds of games and stories to fill the evenings. Not least,
there was sleep, extravagantly long, in the hot, crowded iglu after work
and eating.

Hardened to the cold, Tikigaq hunters were far more preoccupied
with wind and ice conditions than with simple temperature. Light,
too, in the short days, was precious, and every available moment was
harnessed to subsistence.

In the darkness, travellers navigated by the stars, the moon and the
winds and current. Sometimes Tikigaq's lamp-lit skylights could be seen
from the tops of pressure ridges. The movement of the sun, large inshore
ice formations and the coastal hills provided daylight markers. Before
the dawn and after sunset refracted light from the south-east horizon
spread a short, blue dusk. But even in the winter ice-glare often forced
travellers to wear slitted goggles.

The sun disappears at the winter solstice, emerging after ten days'
absence in mid-January. Then, around noon, a shred of light shines on
the southern ice horizon and fades immediately.

An important ritual marked this instant. Soon after solstice, umialiks
awaited the first sunrise of the season. The men rose early. But instead
of walking out to hunt they were joined by their wives on the roofs of
their iglus.

With parka hoods raised against the wind they stood facing south.
Dark blue, Imnat jabbed the horizon. As though breaching from the

sea-ice, the sun would rise there. The first to greet it, *catch* it with their joy-cry –

Ui! Ui!

barked out like a walrus –

would get a whale next season.

Over the next weeks the sun (orange, streaked with scarlet and crimson, distended and misshapen) climbed slowly. Within a month the whole round form had struggled into view. Its disc hugged Imnat.

When the sun had reached this stage the people said, "The sun is leaning on the cliffs! If it wasn't for Imnat, the sun would *katak* [fall]!"

And the sun sister's presence burns sullenly on Tikigaq.
    Here she is again in winter, clambering the sea-ice,
as she climbed into the qalgi,
    mutilated, with her blood and faeces.

"That's Alinnaq's sister showing us her wounds," the people say,
    as she glares at the village across the sea-ice.
Umialiks who have come to greet the sun stand silent.
    Then women who have given birth come out of their iglus.
They stand on the Point with their babies and children.
    When they see the sun rise,
they hold up their babies and make their legs run,
    invoking the sun's energy,
as though calling to their uiluaqtaq sister,
    "Look! we too are women!
We have husbands!
    These are our children!"

Women lift your children!
    Point their legs to daylight!
The sun will make them strong!
    Fast runners! Good hunters!

The Spirit of the Moon and Women

Through autumn and winter,
    when the qalgis were closed,
and frost had scarred the iglu membrane,
    women who had seen the new moon rising
drew its crescent on the skylight window.

Then, wearing a new parka and carrying her pot of water,
    each woman umialik came out of her iglu
and stood on the roof of the entrance-passage
    to call up to Alinnaq, the moon soul, its inua.

"*Tatqim inua*, Moon Soul, Alinnaq!" the women shouted.
    They raised their pots four times to the sky-hole.
"Alinnaq! Alinnaq!"
    raising their pots to the Moon Spirit's iglu,
"Alinnaq! Drop whales in my qattaq!
    Agvaaquktuna: I want to catch a whale!"

A whale's shoulderblade covers the katak in Alinnaq's iglu.
    Every day, he moves the shoulder, just a little.
As the whalebone moves, the katak opens and the moon increases.
    It's full moon when the katak is open.

Samaruna said:
The women raise their qattaqs
and the feathers lift them higher.
When someone's qattaq reaches the moon's katak,
the water in her qattaq fills its katak.
Then the moon drops a whale
through his katak to her qattaq.

Asatchaq:
My mother caught whales that way.
Alinnaq dropped them in her qattaq.
They were whale souls, made of burnt oil.

Samaruna:
That's how Raven Man was made.
The old woman made him out of burnt oil
from the bottom of her oil lamp.

Asatchaq:
After my mother called on Alinnaq,
she found small whales, black ones,
in the water of her qattaq.

She kept them all winter,
in the water of her qattaq, by the oil lamp.
When Alinnaq sent her whale souls,
she and my father always caught a whale next spring.

Samaruna:
But some women can't reach Alinnaq's iglu.
They don't have the power.
These women get nothing.
Their qattaqs stay empty.
And some ask Alinnaq for life.
If their words fly through,
if their qattaqs reach his iglu,
Alinnaq sends life.

Asatchaq:
Alinnaq keeps souls in his iglu on the moon.
Outside, he keeps seals, whales and walrus.
They're in a qattaq by his iglu.
When a woman asks him for a whale.
he picks one from the qattaq by his iglu,
and drops it in the water of her qattaq.

Samaruna:
Inside his iglu, to one side,
Alinnaq keeps caribou and all the land game.
On the other side are life-souls.
When someone is sick and they ask the moon for life,
Alinnaq drops a soul through their iglu skylight.

Asatchaq:
They get well again.

Four Winter Moons before the Whale Hunt

ONE

When the qalgis closed, the first new moon was *Calling through the skylight*. This was when umialik women who'd caught whales the previous year took gifts to their crews' houses. Standing on the iglu roof, they called down through the skylight and gave the women frozen whale meat.

TWO

The next new moon was called *Whittling paddles*. This was when the crews scraped paddles, harpoon shafts and long knife-handles, so all their wooden hunting gear shone clean and new. This pleases the whales. When they look up through the water they will see the skinboat shining.

THREE

At the *Moon for making drag-floats*, umialiks made three sealskin floats for the end of the harpoon line. Each inflated skin was stoppered with a mask they called *inugluk*, "strange human". When a whale dragged the float down the inugluk sang up through the water and told the boat-crew where the whale was.

FOUR

Moon for turning the skin inside-out. Umialiks hung their floats to dry, then half deflated the smallest of the three. This they put on a seal-hunting sled, and the woman pulled it – wearing harness, as though the sled were heavy – to their skinboat. The prow of the boat was raised and set north – the direction that the whales come – and the woman drew the sled beneath it, sang a special song and poured water from her pot on *something between earth and snow*. She then took the float home, calling it "whale meat".

SPRING

Shamans Visit the Spirit Iglu

At the moon before whaling, in early April, all the umialiks send for a shaman. A messenger walks to the shaman's iglu and calls down through the skylight: "*Qamma pigaatin*: You are wanted!"

> *Samaruna:*
> The shaman knows why he is wanted.
> It's time for him to visit the Itivyaaq spirits
> to find out when to start the whale hunt.
> To find how the hunt will go for them.

The shaman takes his drum and walks inland, flanked by the umialik couple. One mile east of Tikigaq they come to the place where the squirrels burrow. This is the Itivyaaq spirit iglu. A whale's vertebra lies on the top of the iglu.

They stop outside the spirit iglu. The woman spreads a skin on the snow, and the shaman starts drumming.

> *Asatchaq:*
> The shaman drums. He goes into trance.
> His soul moves free. It seeks the entrance.
> His soul must pass the vertebra
> that closes the roof of the spirit iglu.

> *Samaruna:*
> The shaman enters. His spirit goes down.
> He dives through the tundra.
> It is hard to get through.
> It is cold and dangerous.
> He enters. He is gone.

> *Asatchaq:*
> The shaman lies on the snow by his drum.
> The umialiks wait.
> His soul is inside.
> The Itivyaaqs expect him.

His soul stands by the inner entrance.
The spirits see him.

Samaruna:
They know why he's come.
They have waited for his visit.

Asatchaq:
The spirit umialik stands next to the bench.
It is Pamiuguksaaq:
the one with the wolftail.
He is leader of the spirits.

Samaruna:
The wolf and the whale are always partners.
Those who please the wolf, the whale will honour.
This is what the stories tell us.

Asatchaq:
Pamiuguksaaq is the leader of the spirits.
And his wife sits on the iglu floor.
She too is powerful.

Samaruna:
There's a third!

Asatchaq:
Yes, a third.
The spirit with the ears is there.
He sits on the sleeping bench.
The long-eared spirit listens to everything.
He listens through the earth.
He listens to what's happening in Tikigaq.

All who break taboo,
who talk, sing, hammer, carve and make a noise
while the shaman is in trance,
the longed-eared spirit hears.
And the spirit also knows
who's eaten unclean food,
and who makes Tikigaq foul
to the approaching whales.

Samaruna:
He listens and he punishes.

Asatchaq:
Under the bench where the long-eared spirit sits,
crawl the souls he has captured.
They are souls from Tikigaq.
The souls of sick people.
When they see the shaman enter,
the souls want him to join them.

Samaruna:
Ii . . . They want him to join them.
But the shaman takes a step.
He steps backward,
and he scrapes his boot.
The souls turn to face him.
Anyone the shaman recognises,
he throws *life* to.
And those who *catch life*,
back in Tikigaq, recover.

Asatchaq:
When the shaman has thrown life,
the spirit with the wolftail speaks.
He will answer questions.
The wolftail spirit makes the north wind blow.

Samaruna:
The north wind is a man.
The north wind keeps the sea-ice open
for the whales to swim through.

Asatchaq:
The south wind is a woman.
When the south wind blows, the sea-ice closes.
Then hunters come in and wait for open water.

Samaruna:
So the shaman asks the wolftail spirit
when the north wind will start blowing.
The spirit tells him.

Asatchaq:
And the woman it is who controls the water.
If Tikigaq has performed its rituals,
if the people are clean and break no taboos,
then the sea will be calm.

Samaruna:
The woman will do this.
The man will make the north wind blow.
But not too much.
Enough to keep the ice from closing.

When all the shamans have visited Itivyaaq, the spirits leave their iglu and themselves go hunting. They leave the earth and make their whale camp off the south side, on the sea-bed. When the spirits are out the shamans and umialiks make a second visit.

Again they walk out. They walk out to the southern sea-ice. When the shaman finds an ice-crack he sits down. He takes his drum and drums until his soul moves free.

Asatchaq:
And when he's in trance,
the shaman dives.
He dives through the sea-ice,
through the water to the sea-bed.

Samaruna:
The Itivyaaq spirits are there already!
They've been out hunting.
They've harpooned a whale!
So when the shaman returns,
he leads the umialiks back to the village.
They go to the umialiks' iglu and call the people.

Asatchaq:
The shaman sits on the passage roof.
He sits on the earth and whalebone rafters.
And when people have gathered,
the woman umialik brings him water.

Samaruna:
It's water from the whale pond.
It's Umigraagvik water,
where a whale came
from a uiluaqtaq's parka.

Asatchaq:
She brings the water in her qattaq.
The shaman drinks.
And then he eats the qattaq.

When everything has gone,
the shaman tells the people
where he's been and the things that he's heard.

Samaruna:
"The Itivyaaq spirits are out already!
They've gone out hunting.
They have caught a whale.

"I have seen them.
I have seen the whale they've taken.
I trod on its flipper.
My boot almost slipped on it!"

Asatchaq:
Then the shaman tells the umialiks how the wind will be.
"Pamiuguksaaq says there'll be a north wind tomorrow.
And the spirit woman wants the sea calm."

The shaman tells them where the boats should go.
And where the sun will rise
when the whales come through.
And what whales they'll catch:
large ones, *usinuaqs,*
or small fat ones, *inutuqs.*

Samaruna:
And they tell them what marks
they'll see on the whales' throats,
how their flippers will appear.

Asatchaq:
The shamans watch the sun.
They watch its progress.
They say which whales will come
when the sun touches Imnat in the morning.
And which whales
when the sun's rim hits the sea horizon.

Samaruna:
When the shamans have spoken,
the umialiks get ready.
Their crews tie their skinboats
to the boat-sleds.

Asatchaq:
The umialiks and their men are ready.
The women lead their boats out.
The whales are approaching.
They walk out to meet them.

THE WHALE HUNT

When the sun came up on the hill called Vertebra and the snow birds were nesting in the village, Asatchaq sang this for the skinboat, which was down from its rack and standing by the qalgi:

Paammaguuq pamma
aanalukpin!
Iqigiin! Iqigiin!

Up there, up there!
Aana's going to beat you![5]
Wake up!
Wake up skinboat!

Samaruna:
The boat has slept all winter.
An old woman will wake it,
It will fly, it will swim
when they take it on the water.

Asatchaq:
At "Covering Boats" moon,
when a north wind blows,
the men build a snow-house by their qalgi.
Here they'll wrap their boat-frames,
with last spring's sealskins.

The dehaired skins have been soaked under sea-ice. The qalgi women sew them into one and cut rope-holds round the edges. When the gunwales have been oiled the men spread the skin and lash it to the boat-frame's horizontals. It dries taut and supple.

Samaruna:
It will fly like a sea-bird.[6]
The skin and skeleton
are light and flexible.
They can never be broken.

Outside each snow-house the umialiks feed the village children.

Asatchaq:
The whales are generous.
Hunters must be generous.
If umialiks share meat
with children and old people,
the whales will approach them.

Samaruna:
Then they call for a child,
and they call an old woman.
"Take this sack.
Go down to *nali!*"[7]

The child walks to the south beach (nali). There he gathers sticks. The men prop the skinboat on its paddles. When the child returns the men build a fire beneath the boat prow.

Asatchaq:
The men light the fire.
The woman approaches.
She stands at the prow.
She sings for the skinboat.

Samaruna:
This makes it fast
and makes it quiet.
The prow has been warmed.
It won't stick to the ice
when the hunters launch it.

The day before they go out on the sea-ice the umialiks wake early and the wife walks to the skinboat.

The woman is wearing wolftail mittens.[8] She sweeps out the boat with her left-hand mitten. Then she lifts her waterpot and pours water on the gunwales.[9]

Then they load the boat with their equipment. Harpoons, lances, spears and cutting tools are strapped to the bottom.

They load lines and drag-floats, grapples, hooks, harpoon blades. The harpooner carries his ivory harpoon rest.

The umialik's amulets are hung from the boat ribs. He has kept the shavings from his shafts and paddles. He takes these with him.

On the morning they go out, the woman calls her crew and feeds them.

Asatchaq:
The men must eat.
The umialiks eat nothing.

Samaruna:
The channel is open.
The spirits have caught a whale already!

Asatchaq:
It is time to go hunting.
The shamans have told them
the spirits' instructions.
The look-out men run home from the sea-ice:

Samaruna:
"*Puiyaqpulguuq!*
Puiyagpulguuq!
The first whales are spouting!
Belukhas are running!"

The men harness themselves to their boat-sled.[10] They are ready to go hunting.

But they wait for the woman. She walks ahead of them. As the men start to pull, the side of the skinboat brushes her parka.

She runs across the men's path. She lets the far side of the skinboat brush her.

The woman leads the skinboat to the south shore. Where the beach meets the ice, again she stops to let it touch her.

Once they've come to the sea-ice the woman falls behind the boat-sled. The husband follows her, always singing. The amulets sewn to their parkas tremble.

The autumn before, during the qalgi rituals, each couple had walked to the Point to look for a crayfish that the waves had stranded.[11] They built a little ice-house and laid the crayfish inside with its head pointing inland. Then they gave it fresh water.

Now, as the crew drags the boat-sled to the sea-ice, they visit their umialik's crayfish iglu.

The husband takes his harpoon and cuts round the ice-house. When they lift the roof off, there's the crayfish!

Ah! Everyone laughs!
The woman rolls the crayfish, belly up.
They laugh again.
It's like a whale.

The skeleton! The skeleton!
    The same thing will happen.
They'll roll the whale over!

The woman lifts the crayfish. She uses her left hand. She carries her pot in her right-hand mitten. When they reach open water the husband takes a thread of baleen, ties the crayfish to a stone and sinks it.

The woman drops her right-hand mitten in the skinboat. It will stay in the boat until the hunt is over. She passes each man her ritual pot. They all drink water.

They have come to the ice-coast through a defile full of pot-holes in a sheltering pressure ridge.

Vast plains of ice-rocks lie behind them. The snow by the channel is fresh and untrodden. Ahead, the sea opens. Tikigaq has vanished.

Secluded from their rivals, the umialiks choose a small bay in the ice-rim. Here they will wait for whales to approach them.

Now they have come the crew is silent. The wife and husband gesture their instructions. The men unload. They slide the skinboat to the ice-rim. The harpoon juts across the water.

When the floats have been rigged to the drag-line, and the drag-line has been coiled, the harpooner climbs in to his front bench. The crew take their places in twos behind him.

The umialik follows. They move off slowly. Ice-floes drift past. They pretend to go hunting.

Alone by the boat-sled, the woman takes her belt off.[12] Still holding her pot, she lies on the ice with her head pointing inland. She waits for the harpooner.

When the men have travelled out some way, they turn the boat and paddle back again. They reach the ice-edge; the harpooner rises.

Samaruna:
The harpooner leans out with his weapon.
The harpooner harpoons her.
He touches her neck
through the hood of her parka.

Asatchaq:
The woman stands up.
She faces inland.
She starts to walk home.

Samaruna:
She doesn't look back.

She leaves her belt.
She leaves her mitten.

Asatchaq:
She walks home to Tikigaq.
When she reaches the qalgi,
She goes to the rack
where the boat lay all winter.

She unlashes the planks and carries them home where she leans them against the iglu passage.

Then she enters the iglu. She hangs her pot above the katak. She lays her mitten by the oil lamp.

Samaruna:
Her husband wears the belt
his wife has left him.
Her right-hand mitten
lies in the skinboat.

Asatchaq:
The wife has not eaten.
Now someone cuts meat for her.
If she cut meat herself,
she would break the harpoon line.

The woman does nothing to frighten the whale or put the boat in danger.

Samaruna:
She does not sew or comb her hair.
She speaks quietly and moves slowly.
She pretends to be sick.
She sits and does nothing.

The sun moves round the hills and over the peninsula. It sets on the western ice-horizon.

The men stand all night in their double parkas. Inside their mittens they wear fawnskin gloves. Their boots are lined with bird's-down and shavings.

Samaruna:
They've thrown their winter clothes out.
They wear new clothes for the whale hunt.

Asatchaq:
The oil and blood on their winter skins
made their old clothes disgusting.

Out of the village the snow is untrodden. The ice is clean. The sea is empty.

The men watch and do nothing. They eat raw meat; they drink cold water.

When they finish their meat the crew's "little muskrat" runs to the village.[13] The muskrat boy is too young to go whaling. He's quick; he's strong. He runs between village and the sea-ice. The hunters need meat. The woman umialik fills the little muskrat's bucket. The boy runs back with it.

The men take their knives. They eat a little. Briefly, in turns, they sleep on the boat-sled.

> *Asatchaq:*
> In the winter we slept.
> If we slept now on the sea-ice
> the whales would pass us.
> We would never see them.

The men wait. They do nothing. They watch the light, they watch the sea. They scan the clouds and the horizon.

Crowds of duck and belukha go through. The men fish for crabs with grids made of baleen. The old men recite the Raven Man's story.

> *Samaruna:*
> Raven killed the first whale.
> The men tell his story
> to make whales come to Tikigaq.

> *Asatchaq:*
> And they tell the story of Aninatchaq.
> Aninatchaq knew when the whales were coming.
> He told his umialik:

> "When the sun touches *Vertebra*
> a whale will come up by your skinboat.
> You will harpoon it."

> *Samaruna:*
> While his men fished for crabs,
> and the sun touched Vertebra,
> this is what happened.

> *Asatchaq:*
> And my grandfather Suuyuk gave me this song.
> It *swept the whales to him:*

Sumun makua tililagich
agvitvichli tililagich
uvuna imma Tikigagmun.

Where shall I tell
the whales to go?
I want to sweep them into Tikigaq![14]

Samaruna said:
These small whales, inutuqs,
small round fat ones
come to us from down there,
from their country south of us.

Asatchaq:
The women sit at home.
They are whale souls in their iglus.
The whales listen and sing.
They hear Tikigaq singing.

Samaruna:
Listen to the north wind!
Listen to the sea-ice!
Listen to the inutuq
rising, breathing!

The boatskin drums,[15] and the swell climbs the ice-rim.
     An inutuq rises. Warm steam drifts across the crewmen's faces.
Aapaah! breathing! *Aapaa!* breathing!
     The harpooner stands. He raises his weapon.
The whale hangs by the skinboat stern.
     Alone in the bow, the harpooner waits to be manoeuvred.
The crewmen freeze.
     The inutuq's back fills the slits in their goggles.[16]
Squatting at the rim, the umialik leans forward
     and works the boat round with a hand and paddle.
As the prow swings in the current tilts it.
     The harpooner stumbles. He trips on the drag-floats.
His elbow strikes the gunwale. He staggers up again and lunges.
     The inutuq dives. The blade stutters and bounces.
The harpooner falls backward. His shaft drops in the water.
     The skinboat pitches.
The crew extend pole hooks, spears and grapples.

The harpooner grabs a paddle and retrieves his weapon.
He turns the boat and sculls back to ice-camp.

Asatchaq:
The children will laugh.
The women will scold him:
"He didn't brace his back leg!"
"The harpooner fell over!"
"He could have struck that inutuq!"
"He should have waited!"

In ecstasy once, the harpooner Kunannauraq,[17]
    woken from his trance of concentration
– eight shamans in one skinboat luring the whale to them –
    hurled his weapon vertically
above the whale that had risen by his skinboat
    – as though Tikigaq itself rose! –
and the harpoon turned, blade downward, diving like a sea-bird,
    planted in its death-place, deep between the vertebrae.

The north wind drops and the channel closes. The men stow their
equipment and drag their boats back.

Samaruna:
Maybe a *south wind* shaman has been singing.[18]
Perhaps someone has tied the ice together.

Asatchaq:
It was the shaman Uqpik who did that.
He fitted four sticks
to the sides of an ice-crack.

Samaruna:
He tied two sticks with men's hair,
and two sticks with women's.

Asatchaq:
That was how Uqpik closed the channel.

Samaruna:
When shamans get angry,
they can stop whales coming.

Asatchaq:
That's what my grandfather Suuyuk did.
He was angry with the people.

He tried to starve Tikigaq.
The umialiks killed him.

The umialiks send for a *north wind* shaman:
   a shaman who loves hunting, and wants to see animals.
The shaman brings his drum and an assistant.
   They sit, and he drums. His soul goes out.
He travels to the sea-bed.
   Some woman lives down there.[19] *She has food. She keeps animals.*
Maybe she'll help them when the shaman has visited.
   Or he goes to the house of the north wind spirit.
He tells the wind's inua:
   "The people are hungry! Tikigaq needs whale meat!"

The wind turns round. The pack-ice retreats.
   They paddle to fresh inlets where the lane is narrow.
Snow settles, clinks, blows on and off the sleeves of their parkas.
   A fog moves in. It is white. There is nothing.
Ducks land in the silence. Blind, they listen.
   "Listen!" Nothing. And then, "Listen." Harsh, long breathing.
The harpooner's right hand grips his weapon.
   A whale has breached. An inutuq is breathing.
The men slide the boat from the green, smooth edge
   the young little muskrat has cleared with his scraper

> *otherwise your aana's*
> *going to beat you.*

Sunk to its handle, the helmsman's long blade stirs the current.
   They labour. They travel. Mush clouds in the water thicken.[20]
The pack is moving. Their wake tumbles between ice-blocks.
   The inutuq breaches. "Ahead. There. By the mush-ice!"
The water heaps, then plunges the skinboat back and downward.
   Up-current, the whale emerges and rolls.
The men on the far side drive their blades through the torrent,
   the near three men, where the inutuq can hear them,
flatten their paddles to the skinboat's belly.

As the whale breathes out, they slacken their paddles.
   The skin shuffles and drags. The beak grinds into ice-mush.
"Young ice!" *Aana's going to beat you!*
   The men back-paddle. The harpooner reaches forward.
He cuts round the prow with the blade of his weapon.

Ahead, the whale escapes under water. It swims underneath.
   The young ice buckles. The skinboat is stranded.

> A bag of young wolf-skulls,
>   a bird's head and a dog's.
> Five red pebbles,
>   and two molluscs his grandfather
> found in a stomach.

> The umialik shakes
>   the sealskin container.
> Its ornaments rattle.
>   The amulets jump.

> He whispers to their spirits:
> *It is now and it was then.*
>   *The animals came.*
> *And now you are coming.*
>   *Right here to us!*
> *Come here to us!* [21]

Under a small board fitted to the prow in front of the harpooner,
   hangs a whale in half-relief, its flippers spread,
tail flush with the board's edge.[22] Modelled from above,
   as if viewed rising through the current, the whale hangs,
unseen, upside-down, back flooded with the grain of water:
   eyes, dark blue trade-beads, pinned blind to each side
of a head traced with one sweep of the carver's burin.
   As though summoning the whale through the plank at his knee,
the harpooner taps sharply on its angled surface.

"*Puġġin agviq!*
Puiġin agviq!"[23]

Rise whale!
Rise whale!

The fog lifts in the silence. The whale has vanished.

> There is waiting. Or there's going round or forcing a way through.
>   There is singing to disperse the ice,
> and there's watching for a lane to open.
>   Drifting across the skinboat's stern,
> the white, older ice moves in and sweeps the mush round them.

The sun climbs. Ducks and guillemots fly rapidly over.
The crewmen rest. It is warm.
    They are locked in their pond of open water.
Their faces are seamed, as they watch the surface,
    by stitches in the boat's reflection.
The umialik gazes round. He laughs.
    His voice climbs steeply, then slants quickly down.
"Maybe since the young ice holds us / we'll wait for the time being."
    A clatter of birds reinforces the silence.

They wait in silence, and the wind is silent.
    Then: "Who has a song?" the umialik ponders.
The mush-ice presses the boatskin through its framework.
    "My song or your father's?" answers a young shaman.[24]
The nose of his mask is a vertical, forked whale's tail,
    raised eyebrows, in the gesture of a *Yes*, are branching whale flukes.
"Put on your mask then," the umialik mutters.
    The shaman's face spins.
The mask-holes eat his eyes and cheekbones.
    The harpooner turns away. "We need that man's paddle.
I'll kill him if he stays out shamanising.
    Kinnaq una! Fool!" he whispers. "Your family is hungry."
Then, "Come back!" he shouts, and lifts his weapon.
    The flukes on the whale-mask slap and go under.
"*Yai!*" from the stern, the umialik counters.
    "All right!" he agrees. "Seven paddles might do it."

The young shaman is still raving.
    The man behind him tears a mitten from his shaman nephew,
and plugs the splashing mouth with dogskin.
    "*Kitaa!* Come on!" The umialik stabs at the slush with his paddle.
The harpooner jumps forward.
    He cuts a triangular section below him.
The men slice down and back with their paddles.
    The boat edges forward.
"*Alla suli!* And another! *Alla suli!*"
    "Like an eight-flippered ugruk!"
"But," smiling at the shaman, "one flipper's missing!"
    "That's the shaman asleep in the ugruk's belly!"

When they reach hard white ice, they drag the boat up.
    The slush drains and they clean their paddles.

The young men take their parkas off and rub snow on their bodies.
　　The older men sleep. They all drink from their pouches.
They've lost the boat-sled. There is nothing to eat.
　　"And our bucket of food!" The umialik laughs.
The shaman sings out: "*Arii!* I'm hungry!"
　　"We thought something ate you!" says his uncle.

The harpooner broods at the skinboat prow.
　　The parchment is scarred, but the stitches and the lashing hold.
Just some of his equipment is disrupted.
　　The broad, thin, slate harpoon blade, with its owner's mark –
in five rhythmical cuts, a quadrangular caribou,
　　tail lifted, two legs visible – has snapped across the middle.
"The nest . . . the nest . . ." the umialik whispers.
　　Wedged in the boat-frame lies his harpoon blade-box:
egg-shaped, the lid studded with a crystal,
　　and bound into place with braided sinew.
The harpooner extracts a fresh slate from the set of five,
　　and tamps down the shavings that pack the remainder.

"Your harpoon rest," the umialik gestures.
　　"I know," he grunts.
"You knocked it. When you fell. The thongs are loose."
　　"I'll tie them."
His left hand raises the two polar bears' heads
　　carved on the shanks of the ivory harpoon rest.
Their eyes are inlaid. Their teeth are serrated.
　　"Your left-handed partner!"[25] he jokes with the umialik.
The white ruff with its bear's snout screens the helmsman's laughter.
　　Two eagles engraved on the stock of the harpoon rest
rear off the boat floor. Their feathers dangle.
　　Each grasps a whale in extended talons.[26]

It is brilliant and windy. Cumulus banked on the white horizon
　　blows south against the movement of the ice-pack.
They coast with the floe drift, then paddle up-current.
　　We're the last of the whale camps. The first run is over.[27]
The umialik scans his men's new fawnskin parka backs.
　　Their long hoods dangle. The wolf ruffs shine.
Everything's too late! too clean!
　　Someone must have struck a whale already.
Each of his boot-legs shows a bleached skin panel.

Even a young man can have three, or even five of those.
Some older umialiks have caught so many –
    a panel for each whale they've taken –
their whole boot-top is bleached sealskin panels.

Still. Yes. Two springs back, when I caught an inutuq,
    all the umialiks raced to claim their own portions.
It was an inutuq, a big inutuvak.
    Who got the first share? It was Aquppak.
(His soul once travelled to the country of the whales.)
    Aquppak's boat lay nearest, and he heard my signal.
All down coast the umialiks followed,
    singing and waving their spears and paddles.
My inutuq dived; it escaped below the shore-fast ice.
    It came up to breathe and we chased the drag-float.
There was oil in the wake. We followed the colour.
    We travelled all night. Then Aquppak passed us.
His harpooner killed it. With one hit, they told me.
    After I'd taken the tail and flippers, and my crew had their portion,
Aquppak won the first share of my inutuq.
(When he'd carried his meat home, he tried to send the ice out.
    We almost lost everything. Aquppak's a shaman.)
Next came Niguvana and his crew. They had lost their harpoon.
    All they had were knives and lances. But they knew how to use them.
Who came third? Qipugaluatchiaq? His first wife was a caribou.
    He turned into a polar bear one winter.
Fourth. It was Piquk. Then came Kakianaq. He died last summer.
    He ate the wrong meat – a pregnant woman gave it to him.
Last came Aqsaqauraq (no one can touch him with a knife or arrow),
    Mammaninna, Isigraqtuaq and cross-eyed Ipiq.
Pauluagana, Nigliq and Nannuna also came: but they got nothing.
    Then old man Aulagruaq arrived. He had only three crewmen.
All the shares had been taken already.
    Who else had a boat? It was Kamik: his first season.
Kamik took a share of Piquk's whale. But he gave it away.
    He carried the meat round and gave it to old people.
Perhaps he'll get a whale next season.[28]

Yes. Six whales were taken.
    The boats from one qalgi didn't get a whale.
That qalgi was Suagvik.
    Their boats got shares from the all others.

Qagmaqtuuq got two whales last season.
It's said that Suagvik took eleven whales one spring.
None of the other houses got one whale between them.

They have come to a place lying west of the peninsula.
    "Down coast! Down wind!" the umialik gestures.
The young shaman drags his blade and then sculls briskly.
    The marks on their paddles have eroded.
"No whale . . . no belukha. The sea is empty."
    They paddle and then drift. They zig-zag south again.
Then: "*Avataqpak*: Drag-float!"[29] the harpooner whispers.
    They hang their paddles and watch the sealskin ride towards
        them.
The young shaman picks his ear with a finger.
    His whale-mask is contorted.
"Listen to the float-mask! Listen to it singing!"
    The harpooner encloses a smile in his mitten.
The men fold their paddles to the skinboat's belly.
    The float bounds closer. It is dark against the water.
First one song, then a second *aya-ya-ya*,
    cross-syncopated from the distance, cross the sea-ice.
"Maybe your cousin Tikiq is a mask-float?"[30]

The harpooner turns to the shaman's uncle.
    "That's Tikiq. And now Aquppak, singing across there."
The umialik tugs an ear and gestures silence.
    The men grip their paddles.
The sealskin scuttles and comes up again.
    The swollen flippers claw the surface.
A big inutuq emerges. It breathes noisily and slow.
    The float-mask with its downturned mouth rolls nearer.
"My cousin Mitik was raped by a float-mask," the young shaman
    stammers.
"Her child was born crazy."[31] The umialik starts counting.
    When I've come to twice fifteen, the whale will rise here.

        Puigin agviq! Puigin agviq!
        Rise whale! Rise whale!

If the whale's not badly wounded, the float may pull the blade out.
    "*Ki!*" he whispers. The skinboat shoots forward.
The drag-float crashes across their gunwales.
    Beneath them the water is full and solid.

Ii! Yes! Old man Tikiq's!
     The float-mask rears. Its mouth is rigid.
I was there in the qalgi when he carved that face disc.
     He brought jade from Kobuk for its eyes and lip plugs.
The boat keel rides the whale's back.
     The whale hangs from their paddles.
The men feel it bursting against their boot soles.

Anaugaa! He hits it. The harpooner strikes downward.
     The blade slits the skin and passes through the blubber.
The hunter twists the hand shaft, and the blade uncouples.
     The broad thin slate reaches down through the muscle.
The foreshaft roots in the clinging blubber.
     The blade runs sideways. It slants along the tissue.
The hand shaft falls across the front two benches.

As the shaft rolls away, the harpooner sings.
     The line must run smooth.
The float must drag the whale back. It must drag it to the surface.
     The harpooner sings downward. Then he spits in the water.
As the line travels out, the song moves with it.
     The hunter spits to make the song go further, travel faster.
That's how I learned it. My uncle taught me. The song went to my mind.
     He put saliva on his finger and I ate it.
That's how I've kept the song he carried.

Quickly the umialik, holding the boat rigid
     with his hand on the paddle, unlashes his boot thongs.
Nothing must be tight and knotted. Otherwise the line will tangle.
     The line rushes out, and the floats jump free.
They fly across the gunwale and hit the water.

The whale rises, and the drag-floats hold it.
     Two harpoon lines stream from the neck skin.
The skinboat pivots. The stern swings across the tail.
     Three men work their paddles.
Three others grab their knives and lances.
     They have long flint pole-knives. They have spears and lances.
Two men stab the whale's cheek.
     "Tail!" shouts the umialik.
"Attack the throat!" the harpooner whispers.
     The whale starts to roll. The stern pitches as the tail emerges.
"Cut the sinew!" The umialik punches.

With a boot on the whale he slashes down and into the tendons.
A man follows with a knife and, staggering across,
   his bench-partner swings his own blade in and sideways.
The tail arches and the flukes slump in the water.
   "Three now! Four spears!"
The head re-emerges. The mouth rotates upward.
   The men fight past each other to the forward gunwale.
They open the throat. They run the breast through.
   "Blood . . . " mutters the young shaman. He sits freezing in
      the middle.
Half out of water, the whale's eye follows the umialik.
   The harpooner chops at the outlet in the whale's breast.
It is sunset. It is many rivers.
   On the convex of the whale's eye, the young shaman sees his
      mask inverted.

It's still breathing! (the umialik).
   "It's trying to breathe. It's still alive!"
The mouth closes, then drops open. Baleen rattles.
   Oil, blood and mucus froth in the blowholes.
It slides along the whale's cheek.
   "*Arii!* it's weeping!"
A plume of blood and water forks across the skinboat.
   There is no inhalation.
                        The singing comes closer.

Tikiq's skinboat appears in the distance.
   We could have eaten that first wound, the umialik ponders.
We could have cut out his harpoon; destroyed the drag-float.
   They say Kamik did that once. Whose whale was it?
He cut out the first harpoon blade, and hid it in his parka sleeve.
   My grandfather told me . . . Yes. It was Suuyuk's. Suuyuk's . . .

But the blade left its owner's mark.
   Kamik kept seeing it.
When he cut into that whale, he saw the owner's mark in it.
   It was there on the skin, on the heart and liver.
He ate the mark. He died that summer.
   The owner's mark got him.

The bow-poles of Tikiq's skinboat lightly bump them.
   Tikiq sits at the stern.
He unhoods and breathes quietly.

His lip-plugs are beads set in mastodon ivory.
He has thin grey whiskers.

The two crews grasp each other's gunwales.
    The two groups gaze into the distance.
Gulls start arriving.
    I've killed this whale. It's old man Tikiq's.
The birds must also have their portion.

Tikiq scans a cloud-bar on the ice horizon.
    "Thank you." His voice stops.
He transfers his paddle.
    "My harpooner struck it. But not hard enough, maybe.
We lost it. Thank you."

Tikiq bends down. He picks something up.
    It is white and oily.
Tikiq throws it. It lands on the whale's back.
    It's the tail of a belukha.
Some old umialiks do that. One day I shall ask him.

"*Ii* . . . Yes . . . Suluk!"
    The old man *names* the younger umialik.
He names him. He laughs softly.
    "We thought you were dead!
Maybe your wife has taken a new husband!"

"We were stranded in the young ice.
    There. On the north side.
It was my fault.
    Here is your whale.
We recognised your drag-float."

"This must be the whale the Moon Spirit sent me."
    Tikiq stands up. He is looking for a bag.
"You get the first share.
    Next year you'll catch your own whale."
"Thank you."

Tikiq bends. He digs in the stern.
    He stands up, holding the skin of a raven.
"We thought your crew had been swept off, and lost."
    He steps out of his boat and displaces the harpooner.
"Someone has been murdered."[32]

Tikiq stands on the whale's head, taking his knife out.
  "It was someone from Katak's boat."
His boots gleam in the bloody water.
  He scratches a section, slices through the skin,
and plunges the raven's head into the blubber.

"Eat!" he murmurs. *That raven was hungry.*

Someone in Katak's boat has been murdered.

Tikiq withdraws the raven's beak.
  It is hot and oily.
He opens the wings.
  He throws one, then the other across his shoulders.
The head wags over the umialik's tonsure.
  The bill scrapes his forehead.

Kaa! screams Raven Man.
Kaa! cries Raven.

Aquppak arrives. Niguvana's boat arrives. Ipiq follows.
  The whale has turned over. It floats on its back.
Five skinboats surround it.
  The men sit and talk quietly.
Tikiq plants a harpoon in the white-blazed chin.
  He fixes a blade for towing the body.
Just like my whiskers . . . "
  Tikiq jerks the hairs between his chin and parka ruff.
"We'll follow," says Suluk.

Each crew fixes a lance in the carcass. The umialiks plant spears in their order of arrival.[33] The five boats link tow ropes. They drag the dead whale to the nearest sea-ice.

Ui! Ui!
  Tikiq leads them.
Tikiq leads the joy cry.
  Ui! Ui!
Suluk leads the umialiks that follow.

When they get to the ice, the men cut off the tail flukes. They strip maktak from the throat and the five crews eat it. When three more boats have come they cut skin and blubber from the stomach. Everyone eats maktak.

Samaruna:
They use someone's foot.
They use the man with the longest foot
to measure their maktak.

Asatchaq:
Only the first eight boats get shares.
The others get something.
But they don't get shares.

They lower the flukes into the first umialik's boat. The men haul the boat to safe, flat ice. Here they'll butcher the carcass.

Samaruna:
They follow the songs
of the first umialik.
They sing as they travel.

When the eight crews get to the butchering site the whale's body is moored to the ice-rim and in turn each umialik with his long pole-knife marks the share he's entitled to.

First they mark the back and top sides. Then they roll the whale over and mark the belly. The first boats get the largest portions. It is divided as follows:[34]

Anirruuk: the whole body from tail to navel. The first umialik takes it.

Avarrak: the two tail flukes belong to the first umialik.

Ini: a strip down the middle of the first umialik's share. It goes to the umialik's shaman.

Taliguk: the flippers are shared by umialiks and crews of the first and second boats.

Qimigluich: the back and sides, from blowholes to mid-tail, is taken by the first umialik's crewmen.

Silviich: the belly and sides surrounding the flippers. This is taken by the second and third boats.

Qaa and *Qaglu:* the lower left-hand jaw is taken by the fourth and fifth boats. The lower right-hand jaw belongs to the sixth and seventh boats.

Tapsinaaq: a strip, one footstep wide, round the whale behind the navel. The eighth boat gets this.

Niksiutaq: the top of the head – all skin and blubber – is shared by everyone. In this way the last boats get a portion.

Tirragiigraq: a triangle of maktak from the bottom jaw. Everyone eats it while they're butchering.

Internal parts: the heart, lungs, liver, tongue, intestines, kidneys, membrane, sinew, jaw-bones, baleen, ribs and vertebrae are taken by the first umialik.

Asatchaq:
This is how the whale is cut
when the first umialik,
over many seasons,
has taken more than five whales.

Samaruna:
But it's different
when the first umialik,
even over many seasons,
has killed fewer than five whales.

Asatchaq:
If he has had fewer than five,
he keeps the tail
and shares it in the autumn.

Samaruna:
Umialiks who've had more than five
share the tail
in late winter, before whaling.

"My wife will be expecting something."
    Tikiq works a pole-knife through the water,
and his man hooks a portion of flipper to the surface.[35]
    They step back on the ice.
The current swings the boat across the whale's side.
    "I shall send Nanmak. He's a fast runner."
Tikiq cores the blubber and slots maktak on to a paddle blade.
    The runner extracts the wife's mitten from the skinboat.
He waits to be sent into Tikigaq, to Tikiq's iglu.

"Ii . . . Yes . . . Suluk . . . " The older man *names* Suluk.
    The name *Suluk* touches him.
His name gently strokes him.

"Send for your wife too."
      The younger umialik looks abashed and down.
All the women will come out on the ice now.
      My wife will come with them.
"Put maktak on your paddle. Send a runner.
      Your wife and mine will greet the whale together."
He is putting me forward. Next winter I'll repay him.

"This is your whale. Your own wife will greet it.
      Your wife will bring the whale fresh water.
My wife will come with the rest of the women."
      "Maybe, then, next spring, you'll get your own whale."

"But since you are sending your messenger to Tikigaq,
      I too will send a runner. He will help bring our sleds out."

The younger umialik returns to his skinboat.
      The men were hungry. They are resting.
The young shaman is slumped on the ice by the skinboat.
      He wakes and his mask rocks, front-down, by his shoulder.

"Ki! Run into Tikigaq. Bring our sleds out!"
      "Arii!" he cries. "But I'm a shaman!"
"Get up. Hurry. How long will the ice wait? I can hear it creaking.
      The whale is hot. It will stink. We want fresh meat.
Its stomach is boiling. Get up. Hurry."
      The umialik turns away. He speaks aloud.
"Perhaps there are other shamans in my skinboat."
      The harpooner is fixing a blade to his weapon.
"Perhaps those other shamans don't say much.
      Perhaps you didn't understand them."
There is laughter from beside the skinboat.
      The shaman hears, but he cannot see.
"Maybe they made this whale approach our skinboat.
      Maybe it was they who brought our share of it."
Up he staggers. He is weeping. "Don't let your eyes freeze."
      "Don't stumble on your lip-plugs," the harpooner shouts after him.
"I knew about it when you told me,"
      the younger umialik gestures down-coast to the lower ice-camps.
"I saw his brother[36] from the distance.
      There was blood on their boat. They were looking for someone."
"You have sent the boy home. You have done well.
      If he had stayed, there would have been fighting.

He is Katak's nephew.
    I was there when it happened.
It was Katak's first whale."
    The older man's voice is flat and boneless.

"I shall tell what happened.
    They were standing together. Nannuna and Katak.
They were standing in his skinboat.
    Katak said: "*Ii* . . . That's my share. But I'll give it away."
That's what Katak said.
    "So mine starts here."
Nannuna said this. I was there. I heard it.
    Maybe Nannuna's knife went too far along the middle.
They couldn't agree where to cut along the middle.
    That's when they started. They wrestled in the skinboat.
Their men were on the ice. They held the skinboat.
    But Nannuna was too old. Katak climbed on top of him.
Nannuna's head was over the benches.
    He tried to get his knife out.
He would have killed Katak. But he couldn't find it.
    Then Nannuna's brother jumped into the skinboat."

The gathered umialiks uneasily listen.
    Tikiq looks down and scrapes a foot. "A hunter must be generous.
He must think of the people. They all have stomachs.
    My crew's stomachs are no larger than the others . . .

"Yes: Nannuna's brother. He jumped in the skinboat.
    But he couldn't do anything.
The boat started rolling. The two men fell over.
    They were both in the water. Katak swam for the ice-edge.
But Nannuna's brother leaned out and grabbed him.
    He grabbed him by the lashings.
Katak's boots were open.
    He'd undone his lashings when he caught the whale.
He tried to reach the ice-edge.
    He tried getting to his people.
But Nannuna's brother held his lashings.
    He dragged him under by the lashings."

It is hot on the ice.
    The two men leave their parkas on the skinboat benches.
They run bare-chested.

Nanmak wears the umialik's mitten.
    He carries the paddle across his shoulder.
        Black skin and white blubber hood the paddle's markings.

Even if the shaman asks me, I shall say nothing.
    I saw what happened.
I was there when Nannuna's brother murdered Katak.
    Katak drowned quickly.
His brother pulled Nannuna from the water.
    They escaped together. They left their skinboat.
They'll have tried to leave Tikigaq before anyone gets them.
    (Katak's brother is a man who never misses.
Last winter he killed Ayuviina with a single arrow.)
    I saw Katak's brother's crew approaching.
There'll be blood on that skinboat.

And this boy who runs beside me:
    some people say he's a genuine shaman –
that he's visited the whaling spirits –
    and flown to the moon's house – masked and unmasked –
talks the spirits' language. I don't know anything.
    Others say he's lazy, crazy – he never goes hunting –
he pretends – he's a liar – wants to be a shaman.
    They say he said this:
that he-was-his-own-mother's-mother-and-that-she-made-Raven,
    and-that-he-was-the-whale-that-Raven-harpooned-when-
Raven-harpooned-Tikigaq.

I say nothing. He is Katak's nephew.
    Why wasn't he in Katak's boat-crew?
Or his older cousin's? They say no one wanted him.
    Then Suluk's boat took him.
He'll go mad when he hears his uncle has been murdered.

The two men follow the boat-sled's trail to Tikigaq.
    There are ponds on the surface.
Snow melts from the ridges and their blue cores glow.
    They climb the south beach. There is grass and driftwood.
Nanmak grips the paddle in the woman's mitten.
    The two runners cross the Point. They run into the village.
It's spring in Tikigaq. It's early summer.
    The longspur, crane and phalarope are here.
The snow birds are warming their eggs already.

The longspurs are nesting on the tundra.[37]
The young shaman disappears.
He'll dive headfirst through his grandmother's skylight.
She lives somewhere on the edge of Tikigaq.
That old aatia's always lived there.
The young shaman has gone. He'll sleep all summer.
The men asked for their sleds.
The young shaman will send his aana's jaw-bones.[38]
They'll use her jaw-bones to drag home their whale meat.

     Nanmak heads for his umialiks' iglu.
        He runs across the Point,
past qalgis and meat racks.
        The dogs stand up.
They jump on their leashes,
        All the dogs are barking.
The children have heard him.
        They rush out barefoot.
He runs with his paddle.
        They race behind him.
They are shouting and laughing.
        "*Qalualuraq! Qalualuraq!*
The runner! The runner!"
        The women come out.
They stand on their roofs,
        they stand shading their eyes
on their iglu passages.
        "It's Tikiq's messenger!
He's caught a whale!
        Tikiq's sent maktak from the flipper!"
Nanmak never stops.
        He reaches Tikiq's iglu.
The snow is thawing.
        He runs up the mound.
There is grass round the skylight.
        He circles the skylight.
Nanmak goes round once,
        in a sunwise direction.
Then he raises the membrane
        at its seaward corner,
and he calls into the iglu:

"Here's fresh maktak!
Here's skin and blubber
from the whale your husband's taken!"
The silence has ended.
The hunt is over.
Tikigaq is noisy.
The women climb out of their iglu passages.
They sing. They shout across the village.
They pick up their knives,
they run to get their sleds and harness.

The women umialiks have been sitting in their iglus.
While the men were on the ice, the women did nothing.
The umialiks come out.
Their sisters and cousins, aunts and mothers,
girls and aanas all come out now.
They've waited quietly in their iglus.
Now the women are laughing. They are ready.

A hand extends from its sleeve to the skylight. It grasps the paddle.
"You have come! It is you!" The woman names Nanmak.
"From Tikiq, my husband! Our boat has been lucky!"
The woman's voice is high and breathless.
The messenger picks off the long oval of maktak.
"*Aarigaa!* Very good! Hand it down! We were hungry for
whale meat!"
It is Tikiq's wife. Sigvana. Tikiq's hunting partner.
"Now everyone can eat. We can all eat maktak!"
Nanmak passes down her wolftail mitten.
He stands at the skylight. The children crowd him.
They swarm round the skylight.
They crane forward on their bellies.
"What kind? How big, Nanmak?" the children whisper.
The woman umialik calls up from the iglu.
"Children! Your *uncle* Tikiq has a whale."
She calls Tikiq their uncle.
"He is with it on the ice. A big inutuq, or an usinuatchiaq.
He has sent me his paddle.
Now I'm going to cook this flipper.
When I come back from the ice, you will all eat maktak!"

Sigvana's voice retreats through the skylight.
It is time to get ready.

She dresses in her ceremonial parka.
　　She dangles the whaleskin over the lamp flame.
The black skin buckles; the fat turns yellow.
　　Oil drips in the lamp bowl.
She sharpens her knife and cuts the maktak into pieces.
　　The boys and young men start arriving.
Each boy has a rule his spirit guardian made him.[39]
　　There are those who eat the first whale of the season.
Others eat the last whale to be landed.
　　Some boys eat seal meat in the morning.
They don't touch whale till the next sun has risen.
　　Some eat fresh whale.
Others eat it aged and frozen.
　　Some boys rub whale fat on their arms and bellies.
Others take it to their guardians.
　　They swallow the meat when their guardians have chewed it.
Some boys eat polar bear, seal and walrus.
　　Their guardians forbid whale in their first twenty winters.

The crewmen's women arrive at the iglu.
　　Sigvana gives them maktak and then kneels by a lamp bowl.
She holds her face above the lamp oil
　　and draws a soot line down her right cheek.
Then she draws soot across the left cheek.

Sigvana puts on her belt and her right-hand mitten.
　　She leaves her iglu with the qalgi women.
The women drag their sleds behind them.
　　Sigvana carries her qattaq of water.
She carries the paddle the messenger brought with him.
　　She has covered the blade-tip with raw caribou stomach.
She carries the last piece of maktak on the stomach.
　　They cross the Point. They walk down the beach.
They leave Tikigaq behind them.

The men stand and wait.
　　The whale floats at the ice-rim.
In turn each umialik
　　stands with Tikiq in his skinboat.
They talk and measure
　　with their feet and pole knives.
The old men advise them.
　　They cut lines along their portions.

Then the men take three paddles
  and they make a tripod.
They lean three paddles,
  blades up, on their handles.
Tikiq binds the paddles,
  then fetches the whale's flukes
and lays them on the sea-ice
  under the three paddles.

Then the women arrive.
  Sigvana arrives with her qattaq and paddle.
She approaches the ice-rim.
  She stands over the whale her husband has taken.
It's the same whale the Moon Spirit dropped in her qattaq,
  last winter when she came out on her iglu passage.
Sigvana raised her qattaq, with the other women, through the
          sky-hole.
"Alinnaq!" she shouted. "Drop a whale in my qattaq!"
  She kept her qattaq in the iglu by the katak.
She kept the whale that the Moon Spirit gave her.
  Then she sat in her iglu. She did nothing.
While the men were on the ice, she sat and did nothing.

That's how they caught it.
  She sat at home and lured the whale to her.
She sat in her iglu, in the *animal*,
  till her husband harpooned it.
She and her husband will send it to Tikigaq.
  They'll store its meat in the *animal*'s body,
in the animal that Raven killed, whose body became Tikigaq.

Sigvana arrives with the qalgi women.
  She wears her ceremonial parka.
She hands back the maktak.
  She gives them the paddle.
The men slice up the maktak with the stomach.
  The crew eats maktak and caribou stomach.
Then the men cut holes in the ice near the water.
  They thread the holes with sealskin rope,
and raise the whale's head to the ice-edge.
  When the head is on the ice, Sigvana lifts her qattaq.
"Ii! Yes! *Quyanaq! Ii!* Yes! Thank you!"

She cries "Quyanaq! Thank you!
You have come to my husband!
You have come to our qalgi!
You have come to join our people!
You have come to Tikigaq!"

Sigvana lifts her qattaq.
    She pours water on the whale's head.
She gives the whale a drink of water.
    The water comes from a pond in Tikigaq.
The umialiks chopped ice there.
    Their wives kept it all winter.
A man made a whale there
    with a caribou-skin parka.
It was soaked in the blood
    of a woman who won't marry.
The men raped her in their qalgi.

She pours water in the whale's mouth.
    She pours water in the blowhole.
It is water from land.
    It is Tikigaq water.
She talks to the whale's soul.

            "You died at sea!
            Your soul must be thirsty!
            Thank you for joining us!
            Here is water!"

Sigvana has finished.
    She lays her qattaq on the whale flukes
under the three paddles.
    She takes off her parka
and covers the paddles.

She walks to the skinboat
    and takes her husband's amulets.
She picks up the masks,
    the wolf-skulls and the effigies.
She lays the amulets over her parka.

The men turn to the whale.
    They sharpen their knives.
They get their meat hooks ready.

They start butchering the whale.
The whale's body is dismembered.

Samaruna:
The whale hunt has finished.
The ice is floating north again.

Asatchaq:
While the men cut the whale,
the boys and women drag meat to Tikigaq.

Samaruna:
They open their caches.
They line their old iglus.

Asatchaq:
The women start cooking.
They cook maktak for their qalgi.

Samaruna:
The children come first.
They run to their umialiks' iglus.

Asatchaq:
The children struggle at the skylight.
They throw soot at one another.[40]
    Samaruna:
The children drop spits
and pull maktak through the skylight.

Asatchaq:
Out on the ice the men finish cutting.
They haul the ribs and jaw-bones back to Tikigaq.

Samaruna:
The umialik cuts the whale's head.
He cuts it from the final vertebra.

Asatchaq:
The men cry out.

Samaruna:
The skull meets the water.

Asatchaq:
The whale's soul escapes.
It returns to its country.

Samaruna:
They have finished.[41]
They are happy.
It will find a new parka.

Asatchaq:
"Come again!" shouts the Raven.
The women repeat it.

GLOSSARY

Spelling is in standard Inupiaq (north Alaskan Inuit) but with diacritical marks omitted. The pronunciation of most vowels and consonants is equivalent to the English. But:

Vowels

Short *a* is like *u* in "cut".
Short *i* is like *i* in "pin".
Short *u* is like *oo* in "soot".
Short *u* before *q* or medial *g* is like *o* in "hot".
Short *i* before *q* or medial *g* is like *e* in "wet".
Long *a*, as in "aana", is like short *a* but lengthened and stressed.
Long *i*, as in "ii", is like short *i* but lengthened and stressed.
Long *u*, as in "avataliguuvaq", is like short *u* but lengthened and stressed.
All diphthongs receive stress, as in *aa*na, in*u*a, p*u*iya, um*ia*lik.

Consonants

q is a uvular stop, like a *k* pronounced at the back of the throat. The medial *g*, as in "Tikigaq", is pronounced like a French *r*.

aana (ahnu)*	grandmother
agviq (urvek)	whale
anatkuq (ungutkok)	shaman
anaq (unuk)	excrement
avataliguuvaq (uvu-tuli-goovuk)	snow bunting
avataqpak (uvutukpuk)	float for whaling harpoon
iglu (igloo)	semi-subterranean winter house
igniruaqtuqtuq (er-ni-rawk-toktok)	amulet associated with birth-things
inua (in-yoo-u)	1) resident spirit 2) "human" component in animal soul structure
inugluk (inyorlook)	mask fitted to avataqpak

* Rough pronunciation is given in brackets.

Inupiaq (Inyoopiuk)	north Alaskan Inuit, Eskimo
Ipiutak (Ipyutuk)	pre-Inupiaq village on Tikigaq Point
Itivyaaq (Itivyaahk)	whaling spirit place and spirit person
katak (kutuk)	iglu entrance-hole
maktak (muktuk)	whaleskin with blubber attached
nali (nulli)	Tikigaq's south shore
natchiq (nutchek)	hair seal
nigrun (nerroon)	animal; name for Tikigaq
nuna (noonu)	land
nuvuk (noovook)	point of land
puguq (poogok)	ceremonial carving made annually
puiya (pooi-yu)	lamp residue
qalgi (kul-gi)	ceremonial house
qanitchaq (kunitchuk)	entrance passage
qattaq (kuttuk)	waterpot
qilya (kel-ya)	shamanic power
qugvik (korvik)	wastepot
quluguluguq (kolorolorok)	old ceremonial carving
qunuqtuqtuq (kong-ok-toktok)	amulet associated with grave goods
taimmani (taym-muni)	back then
taqsiun (tuk-siyoon)	lure song for land animals
tatqiq inua (tutkem in-yoo-u)	moon spirit
tulugaq (tooloowak)	raven
tupitkaq (toopitkuk)	shaman's magical familiar
ugruk (oogrook)	bearded seal
uiluaqtaq (weel-yawk-tuk)	literally: "woman who won't take a husband"
ulu (ooloo)	semi-lunar woman's knife
umialik (oomaylik)	male or female skinboat owner
unipkaaq (oonipkahk)	old story
uqaluktuaq (okalooktawk)	ancestor history
usuk (oo-sook)	penis
utchuk (ootchook)	vagina
yugaq (yooguk)	amulet dances

NOTES

PROLOGUE

1 Aana stories typically show the old woman on the outskirts of an unspecified village living with an "orphaned" grandchild. Grandmother-and-child (*aanagiik*) have no other family, so the boy goes begging or hunts to feed his aana. The story here conforms to pattern. Most versions have the aana living with a grandson at the outset; in this tale the boy is subsumed into the persona of the aana's Raven creation. As in other aanagiik stories Tulunigraq leaves home and travels round to "fix things up". This means killing *inuas* (destructive monsters) and putting the final touches to the half-formed primal order. From the moment the boy leaves her iglu the old woman drops out of the narrative. The boy's successes nonetheless derive in part from the grandmother's magic and the power that resides in the aanagiik duo.

2 Uiluaqtaq stories develop the aanagiik pattern. Sewing or combing, the magical virgin lives alone in her iglu. When suitors appear, she kills them, often using the comb which is her shamanic power object. This disequilibrium between the sexes is brought into balance by an "orphan" who has left his aana. The boy is impervious to uiluaqtaq magic. His own shamanic power derives from his part in the aanagiik relationship. The orphan forces the female counter-shaman to marry him and thus neutralises her destructive magic. Together the couple becomes *nuliagiik* (a wife-and-another) in contrast to both partners' previous isolation and the uiluaqtaq's negativity. Just as the old woman in her iglu is a benevolent inua, informing earth with creative energy, so the uiluaqtaq, like the other monsters the young shaman destroys, is a malevolent inua.

In Tulunigraq's story, the first inua that Raven defeats is the uiluaqtaq. While it was the grandmother who empowered this first conquest, it is now the wife's turn to add shaman power to Raven's; the death of the sea beast is their dual accomplishment.

I. TIKIGAQ: WHALE

1 A Tikigaq audience would have noted three main points. First, that someone should successfully achieve the almost impossible journey between Tikigaq and East Cape Siberia – twice. Second, that Migalliq wasn't, in line with custom on both sides, killed by his hosts. Third, that Siberian people should be so foolish as to hunt the grey whale in preference to the meatier, fattier and more docile bowhead. They would have also taken pleasure in Migalliq's ambiguous trade deal. Copper, obtainable occasionally from metal workers of the distant Siberian interior, had largely magical, talismanic value. Tikigaq would therefore prize it greatly. And while Tikigaq hunters might, for both ritual and pragmatic reasons, sincerely give preference to sharp, dispensable slate harpoon heads, the bargain was Migalliq's. For although Uluurat, where he met the Siberians, represents an outcrop of slate only about thirty yards long, there was plenty there, and at other sites, for everyone.

2 The low, rolling contour of the Point is thus spiked with wood and whalebone verticals. A Tikigaq legend has it that the Point was once forested. A man, his wife and only son lived there. When the son died suddenly the man, in grief, hurled his caribou-skin glove at the trees, and destroyed them all for ever. By coincidence, the word *tikigaq* means "forest" in the Kobuk River valley, 130 miles south of Tikigaq.

3 In Rasmussen (1952).

4 Told by Colville River people, north Alaska; in ibid.

5 In Rasmussen (1930).

II. THE RITUAL YEAR

1 Bob Tuckfield, 1973, and in Rasmussen (1974).

2 In Rasmussen, ibid.

3 The image of the string game or string figure runs through the book in two main forms. First, there are the figures themselves whose construction was in harmony with Inuit knowledge of anatomy and the way people made their weapons and equipment. This knowledge of articulation was of special importance to Tikigaq hunters. The composite structure of weapons, traps, and much ritual equipment was modelled on the way that bodies are jointed. Parallel to this and to string-game symbolism were the etched magical diagrams that showed animal silhouettes filled with "X-ray" skeletons

or a horizontal "lifeline" which represented a "string" of the soul element.

An important three-dimensional version of these allusions to body and spirit was the string game – cat's cradle – which was often accompanied by songs and stories. The medium was a loop of sinew or skin cord whose patterns were developed in two phases. The first was a slow, deliberative weaving in which the outer frame was constructed. This was followed by a series of manipulations which filled the structure with lines, rings, knots and nooses, each part of which was sufficiently tense to stay in place, while flexible enough for the next transformation.

Flicking and scrambling through each minutely controlled sequence, the fingers created a series of narrative concatenations. Each movement of the diagram had its moment of identity. The forms that hopped, twitched and ran up and down the frame were semi-abstract narrative animations. Most string games showed animals in archetypal, often comic situations. Small creatures confronted larger species. Mythic archetypes were guyed and inverted as in this scatological allusion to Tikigaq's myth pattern: *"An aana lived with her grandson. They lived in an anus. The grandson said, "Get me some meat!" "All right," said the aana, and out she went to the edge of the anus."*

In the animal stories, the impact of one character on another or with the intractable world was usually sudden and brutal, as in the owl's proposal to the bunting. In others, for example, a lemming loses its footing on an iglu skylight; a squirrel lures a brown bear on to river ice too thin for its weight. Once the order of things has been subverted, the scene dissolves and the string hangs loose.

Creatures in conflict or simply at large in their places: all these were diagrammed. But play was brief and, although often technically spectacular, somewhat casual. Like animals that pop up and then vanish, string-game creatures briefly came to life and then melted away.

As elsewhere among Inuit, the construction of string figures was attended by taboo. They were not for example to be made in the summer; they must not be touched by moonlight. This avoidance suggests fear that the sun and moon spirits would be jealous of mimetic creativity. And whether in the hand of a child or an adult the string game was a shamanistic process. Just as shamans constructed magical familiars from dead material and sang life into it as they went, so string-game players hummed over their making, and a creative and destructive process was enacted.

As the rituals of Part Two show, strings, cords and thongs wove through the village in ways that were equally non-utilitarian. Gifts were strung on cords at the dances; children hung strings through the iglu skylight to be spitted with meat; meat was pierced with strings on a journey to a sacred pond; trade effigies were displayed on cords; and at one of the most solemn moments of the autumn rituals, sacred carvings were hung on thongs from qalgi ceilings – this latter representing a version of Tikigaq's cosmos that hung above rituals that were in themselves a tacked-together sequence. As people threaded across Tikigaq to visit rival houses, compete in games, to dance and to be feasted, the whole village was connected in a rivalrous, mobile pattern. String games evolved in the palms of the player. Between the qalgis and inside their walls, the metaphor was physically embodied.

4   In Rasmussen (1930).

5   The presence of aana, the earth crone who made Raven, lies at the inception of the whole mythologised whaling enterprise. The aana is invoked both for her archaic magic and to ensure the hunt's decorum.

6   This line is taken from a Tikigaq story.

7   The south beach was both a driftwood deposit and the gateway to the whale. The sun and migrant species come from the south. Nali was also the path child shamans took on their journeys.

8   For wolf and whale symbolism, see pp. 65 ff.

9   For the waterpot, see pp. 96 ff.

10 Dogs were too noisy and too valuable to be taken on to the ice. And while dog and wolf amulets were used at whaling, the dog was also, paradoxically, unclean, and would pollute the sea-ice.

11 I have assumed here that the appearance of the crayfish is homologised with a vision of the whale's skeleton. But the comic symbolism, so frequent in animal tales, of small animal versus large partner/ enemy may also be here.

12 This ritual, and the woman's actions that follow, is discussed on pp. 41–42 ff.

13 I have omitted a qalgi ritual that may be connected with this nickname. At the end of the autumn at least one of the qalgis strung ropes across the ceiling. A stuffed marmot was "brought to life" along one of the lines and made to chase suspended whale bladders. The bladder was said to contain an aspect of the whale's soul. Muskrat and marmot are both inland animals. As with the crayfish symbol there is counterpoint of little and large, absurd and majestic. The "little muskrat" scuttles between village and whale camp. He is, as it were, on a line between two centres. He's a necessary provider, but hierarchically low. Like the destitute child who becomes a

shaman, the little muskrat will one day be umialik.

14 The historical Asatchaq recorded this song twice. He attributed it both to his great-grandfather Suuyuk, and to Mannuyaaluk, both mid-nineteenth-century shamans.

15 Early in the season some boats wait for inutuq whales to rise in small calm bays. The narrative that follows, with its accumulating then dissolving individual focus, is fiction.

16 To avoid snow blindness everyone wore slitted goggles made of wood or ivory.

17 A harpooner of early this century. I have translated the incident to the pre-contact period.

18 Sometimes people attributed south wind to the malevolence of shamans; some shamans specialised in raising a particular wind. For stories of other shamans who interfered with whaling, see Lowenstein (1992), stories 12, 20, 24.

19 The all-powerful Canadian and Greenlandic Inuit sea deity Nuliayuk or "Sedna" is a shadowy presence in Tikigaq lore. She is vaguely represented by a "woman in the sea they call *niggivik* (place of food)". See ibid., commentary to story 1.

20 Mush-ice forms and sometimes sets in open water during variable spring weather. Too soft to walk on and too thick for travel, it can maroon a skinboat.

21 The song is by the writer, not recorded.

22 Bench-shelves often had such carvings.

23 I have transposed a seal song to a whale song by substituting agviq for natchiq (seal). This was one of Asatchaq's lure songs.

24 The umialik has not spoken, but the shaman answers. The young man's status is ambiguous. The qalgi rituals and the hunt are a vast collective shamanic event. But not everyone liked or even believed in the shamans themselves, and as stories attested there were plenty of frauds alongside genuine initiates. The young man's apparent and unhelpful pretension thus elicits scepticism. As the umialik later suggests, there may be other shamans in the skinboat maintaining a contemptuous discretion or practising in secret. But the vein of scepticism and the feeling of unease that some shamans prompted cannot be taken at face value. As Nanmak later suggests, the young shaman may belong to the company of mythic "poor boys" who in stories co-existed with historically credible Tikigagmiut. The whale mask with its tail-fluke nose and eyebrows is likewise a prop which the young man projects from phantasmagoric thought.

25 Polar bears hunt seals at ponds and breathing holes with the front left

paw. *Partner* connotes amulet animal, spirit partner.

26 See p. 102 for a short account of the whale-hunting eagle.

27 The chronology that follows is condensed, to suggest that they are quite near the end of the six-week season.

28 See Lowenstein (1992), stories 12, 7, 15.

29 Someone to the south has harpooned a whale. It has escaped with harpoon and drag-float. The whale "belongs" to the first-strike umialik. Each boat that strikes subsequently will get a share.

30 This means "index finger" and is a common Tikigaq name. In the course of writing I landed on this name after several trials. Though perhaps too appropriate for the "perfect" and judicious umialik, the name stuck, and I've kept it. None of the other names is symbolic, though Suluk ("feather") was chosen for its silky texture: the youngish, somewhat insecure umialik, being *stroked* with his own name by Tikiq (p. 143). Most Tikigaq names, including Samaruna and Asatchaq, are archaic and have lost any denotation.

31 A nineteenth-century woman, Mitiktaun, was said to have been raped by a mask called Qaaqpanaaq.

32 Just as the chaos of the first hunting episodes is in counterpoint to the formality and control of ritual, so the murder punctuates the controlled joy of umialik co-operation.

33 The whale is marked with dividing lines later. In the meantime, each umialik identifies the area of his portion with a walrus spear. The spear-stuck whale becomes a kind of puguq, ritual object.

34 This schema is approximate. All sources, from 1940 to 1980, differ as to the exact division. Around 1940 an umialik brought his colleagues together to try re-establishing the pre-contact system. Share allocations may, however, have varied according to generation, and even within the same period. This in itself may have accounted for some inter-umialik disputes.

35 The tail flukes and flippers were part of the first umialik's share. The meatless, boneless maktak is tough and thin. The contrast of black skin and white blubber is echoed in the graphite paddle symbol. Slices of flipper are fragrant and hard to chew. They have ritual prominence and are eaten in small quantities.

36 Kisuatchiaq, the murdered man's brother. As he walked home Nannuna saw Kisuatchiaq's boat approach round an ice-block. Nannuna told Kisuatchiaq he had fallen in the water and was on his way home to fetch dry clothing. Kisuatchiaq, a strong man, was suspicious. He sent his boat on and stayed with Nannuna. As Kisuatchiaq turned to watch his boat disappear, Nannuna struck

him in the back with a pole-knife. Kisuatchiaq died instantly. The feud continued.

37 The whale hunt started when the snow buntings arrived. The arrival of the Lapland Longspur marked the end of whaling.

38 The detail is from an aana-and-orphan story told by Asatchaq in 1976.

39 Though Tikigaq broke and re-arranged widespread taboos against combining foods from the sea and inland, men often spent their first twenty years in strict taboo relationship with whale meat.

This would put them in ritual harmony with the whale by the time they were members of a skinboat crew.

40 The final allusion to Raven's creation story. See pp. 60–61.

41 As the final line suggests, the cycle is not over. The process is left hanging between accomplishment and expectation.

SOURCES

The book derives from fieldwork in Point Hope between 1973 and 1989, and experience of the whale hunt over three seasons, 1975–77. Most of the stories were recorded in Point Hope between 1973 and 1980; with one or two exceptions they were recited in Inupiaq and translated by Tukummiq, a bilingual Tikigaq woman, and myself. As mentioned in the Acknowledgments, my account of qalgi rituals in Part Two is based largely on the unpublished field notes of Froelich Rainey, 1940. With the exception of the two origin myths which appear in my book *The Things that were Said of Them*, and the texts from Rasmussen, all the stories were recorded during fieldwork and are printed here for the first time.

I should perhaps again underline the separation between the stories and my own poetry. My effort has been to reconstruct an old religious drama and to show how people lived within the structure of its poetic idea. Every ritual or subsistence act is a part of the "poem" within whose sphere the community lived. Local stories embody their own poetry. My own contribution is simply an attempt to encapsulate or interpret in a Western idiom experience which may lie under or parallel to the narrative genre.

The narrative of the hunt itself is a fusion of various skeins. The setting on the ice is as I experienced it in the mid-1970s. The *dramatis personae* are imaginary, although the histories of Nannuna and Kunannauraq are as recorded in Tikigaq. Within bounds anything might happen at whaling. Most of the village-based rituals take place in orderly sequence within the control of human agency. Once the hunt takes off, and the men are confronted with forces beyond their control, ritual hierarchies may be thrown off-centre for a time. Sacred practice thus partly gives way to demands of character and situation.

STORY SOURCES:

How Raven Man was Made, p. 3: Umigluk, March 1975
How the Whale became Land, p. 5: Asatchaq, December 1975
Sun and Moon story, p. 10: Asatchaq, December 1975
"Migalliq was a Tikigaq hunter", p. 24: Sagana, June 1981
"Long ago when a man", p. 29: Tigluk, July 1977

"The one-legged shaman", p. 30: Asatchaq, January 1977
"While the men were on the cliffs", p. 34: Asatchaq, April 1976
The Raven and the Whale, p. 38: Rasmussen, 1952
"The souls of two shamans", p. 40: Rasmussen, 1952
The Whale-float in the Iglu, p. 41: Asatchaq, March 1976
A Whale Harpooned in the Iglu Katak, p. 43: Asatchaq, June 1976
A Shamaness Raises a Whale, p. 43: Asatchaq, June 1976
The Drum in the Katak, p. 45: Rasmussen, 1952
Snow-bird story, pp. 49–50: Qimiuraq Bob Tuckfield 1973 and
    Rasmussen 1974
Lemming story (*Alla suli*), p. 50: Rasmussen 1974
"This is the path", p. 52: based on stories from Asatchaq 1976
"Two men, they say", pp. 53–54: Piquk 1977
Daylight and Darkness, p. 58: Asatchaq
How Raven became Black, pp. 60–61: Rasmussen 1930
Qiikigaq and Qiikiaaluk ("This story is about a wolfskin"),
    pp. 66–68: Asatchaq, January 1977
"Before leaving the village", p. 69: Asatchaq, 1976
"I belonged to Unasiksikaaq", pp. 79–81: based on rearranged
    fragments, 1976
Lemming story, pp. 82–84: Umigluk 1975 and Tigluk 1989
Raven and Snowy Owl, p. 83: Umigluk 1973
Lemming and Shrew, p. 85: Asatchaq 1976
Seagull story, pp. 85–86: Asatchaq 1976
Uiluaqtaq story, pp. 99–100: Asatchaq 1976
Eagle Girl story, pp. 102–103: Asatchaq 1976
What the Whales Do, pp. 103–104: Qimiuraq Bob Tuckfield 19 73
Katak and Nannuna, p. 145: Rainey 1940, Asatchaq 1976

The translations are by Tukummiq and Tom Lowenstein.

SELECT BIBLIOGRAPHY

Bonner, Nigel *Whales* (London, 1980)

— *Whales of the World* (London, 1989)

Burch, Ernest S. *The Traditional Hunters of Point Hope, Alaska, 1800–1875* (North Slope Borough, Barrow, Alaska, 1981)

Carroll, G. M. "Bowhead Whale Feeding near Point Barrow", *Arctic* 40 (2) (1987)

Dorsey, E. M. "Factors Affecting Surfacing, Respiration and Dive Behaviour in the Bowhead Whale", *Canadian Journal of Zoology* 67 (7) (1989)

Eschricht, D. F. and Reinhardt, J. *On the Greenland Right Whale* (London, 1866)

Everitt, R. D. "Sexual Behaviour of the Bowhead Whale", *Arctic* 32 (3) (1979)

Foote, Don Charles *Eskimo Hunting of the Bowhead Whale at Point Hope, Alaska* (Foote Collection, University of Alaska Archives, Fairbanks, 1962)

— *Observations on the Bowhead Whale* (Fairbanks, 1964)

George, J. C. "Observations on the Ice-breaking and Ice Navigation of Migrating Bowhead", *Arctic* 42 (1) (1989)

Haley, D., ed. *Marine Mammals of the Eastern North Pacific* (Seattle, 1978)

Herman, Lewis M. *Cetacean Behaviour* (New York, 1980)

Larsen, Helge and Rainey, Froelich "Ipiutak and the Arctic Whale Hunting Culture", in *Anthropological Papers of the American Museum of Natural History* (New York, 1948)

Lowenstein, Tom unpublished field notes and recordings from Point Hope, 1973–89

— *Sea Ice Hunting in Point Hope* (North Slope Borough, Barrow, 1981)

— *The Things that were Said of Them: Shaman Stories and Oral Histories of the Tikigaq People* (University of California Press and Douglas & MacIntyre, 1992)

Nelson, E. W. *The Eskimo about the Bering Strait* (US Bureau of American Ethnology, Washington, 1899)

Nelson, Richard *Hunters of the Northern Ice* (University of Chicago Press, 1969)

Pulu, Tupou; Ramoth-Sampson, Ruth; Newlin, Angeline; Frankson,

David; and Frankson, Dinah *Whaling: A Way of Life* (National Bilingual Materials Development Centre, Anchorage, n.d.)

Rainey, Froelich unpublished field notes from Point Hope, Archives of the University of Alaska, Fairbanks, 1940

— *The Whale Hunters of Tigara*, Anthropological Papers of the American Museum of Natural History (New York, 1947)

Rasmussen, Knud *Across Arctic America: Narrative of the Fifth Thule Expedition* (New York, 1927)

— *Intellectual Culture of the Iglulik Eskimos*. Report of the Fifth Thule Expedition 1921–24, vol. 7, no. 1 (Copenhagen, 1930)

— *The Netsilik Eskimos: Social Life and Spiritual Culture*, Report of the Fifth Thule Expedition 1921–24, vol. 7, no. 1 (Copenhagen, 1931)

— *The Alaskan Eskimos, as Described in the Posthumous Notes of Knud Rasmussen*, Report of the Fifth Thule Expedition 1921–24, vol. 10, no. 3 (Copenhagen, 1952)

— *Eskimo Poems from Canada and Greenland*, trans. Tom Lowenstein (London, 1974)

Ray, Dorothy Jean *Eskimo Masks: Art and Ceremony* (University of Washington Press, 1967)

— *Eskimo Art: Tradition and Innovation in North Alaska* (University of Washington Press, 1977)

Scammon, Charles M. *Marine Mammals of the Northwestern Coast of North America* (New York, 1874)

Scoresby, W. *An Account of the Arctic Regions with a History and Description of the North Whale Fishery* (1820)

Spencer, Robert F. *The North Alaskan Eskimo* (Smithsonian Institution, 1959)

Vanstone, James *Point Hope: An Eskimo Village in Transition* (University of Washington Press, 1962)

Wursig, B. "Feeding, Aerial and Play Behavior of Bowhead Summering in the Beaufort Sea," *Aquatic Mammals* 15 (1) (1989)